Insects & Bugs for Kids

BUTTERFLIES, BEES, AND MORE

An Introduction to Entomology

Jaret C. Daniels

Adventure Publications
Cambridge, Minnesota

ACKNOWLEDGMENTS

I would like to thank my loving wife and best friend, Stephanie, for her unending patience, sense of humor, and support. She makes our life together truly wonderful. I also want to thank our many doting cats. They regularly keep me company during projects like these and quickly alert me should any of the assorted insects in our home escape. Lastly, I wish to thank my parents for encouraging my early interest in the natural world. It resulted in a continuously rewarding and always surprising career.

Disclaimer Kids should always be accompanied by an adult when outdoors, and it's your responsibility to recognize, and avoid, the potentially dangerous bugs, insects, plants, or animals in your area. Always be aware of the weather and your environmental surroundings, and stay off private property. Finally, don't handle bugs or insects unless you're certain it's safe to do so.

Edited by Brett Ortler

Cover and book design by Jonathan Norberg

Cover photos: **ArtLovePhoto/Shutterstock:** Mosquito; **Eric Isselee/Shutterstock:** Grasshopper; **Fotofermer/Shutterstock:** Inchworm; **Frode Jacobsen/Shutterstock:** Eastern Tailed Blue Butterfly; **JanyaSk/Shutterstock:** Grass Background; **Jay Ondreicka/Shutterstock:** Monarch Chrysalis; **Jonathan Norberg:** Hand; **junrong/Shutterstock:** Stink Bug; **Khairil Azhar Junos/Shutterstock:** Monarch; **khlungcenter/Shutterstock:** Firefly; **Macronatura.es/Shutterstock:** Asian Beetle; **Melinda Fawver/Shutterstock:** Spider and Walking Stick; **Nataliia K/Shutterstock:** House Fly; **Picture Partners/Shutterstock:** Earthworm; **Sari Oneal/Shutterstock:** Eastern Black Swallowtail Butterfly; and **sruilk/Shutterstock:** Ants.

All photos copyright by Jaret Daniels unless otherwise noted.
Scott Bauer, USDA Agricultural Research Service, Bugwood.org: pg. 79 (bottom); **Warren P. Lynn:** pg. 68 (bottom); and **Brett Ortler:** pp. 108, 114 (all), 117, 118; **Stephanie Sanchez:** 128

credits continued on page 127

10 9 8 7 6 5 4 3 2 1
Insects & Bugs for Kids

Copyright © 2021 by Jaret C. Daniels
Published by Adventure Publications, an imprint of AdventureKEEN
310 Garfield Street South
Cambridge, Minnesota 55008
(800) 678-7006
www.adventurepublications.net
All rights reserved
Printed in the United States of America
ISBN 978-1-64755-164-3 (pbk.); ISBN 978-1-64755-165-0 (ebook)

Insects & Bugs for Kids

BUTTERFLIES, BEES, AND MORE

An Introduction to Entomology

Table of Contents

All About Bugs

If you want to observe or study bugs, it helps to know a bit more about them first. The term "bug" is generic and typically refers to a wide assortment of small, creepy-crawly critters. All bugs are **arthropods** (say it, *ar-thro-pods*). Arthropods are invertebrates—they don't have an internal skeleton and bones. Instead, they have an external skeleton, a segmented body, and jointed appendages, such as legs and antennae. The arthropods are a large group of animals that includes insects, crustaceans, spiders, centipedes, millipedes, and scorpions. Together they are the largest, most diverse and widespread group of animals on the planet, representing nearly 85 percent of all known animal species.

ARTHROPOD EXAMPLES

Jumping Spider (spider)

Pillbug (crustacean)

Millipede (millipede)

Stone Centipede (centipede)

Monarch Butterfly (insect)

Insects are by far the most familiar and frequently encountered arthropods. They are also incred ibly diverse, with over 1 million known species. The vast majority of species on Earth that are yet to be described are likely insects and other arthropods. In fact, scientists conservatively estimate that the total number of insects could exceed 8 million when all are eventually discovered. While the vast majority of that amazing diversity exists in the tropics, there are well over 150,000 species of insects in the United States and Canada alone. They are also incredibly abundant. Although it may sound crazy, there are about 1.5 billion insects on Earth for every human being.

Entomology (say it, *ent-o-mall-o-gee*) is the study of insects. It is a big scientific field that makes contributions to biology, agriculture, chemis-try, human and animal health, conservation, the environment, medi-cine, and even criminal investigation (forensics).

Some insects, such as Tomato Hornworms (a moth caterpillar), can cause damage to plants or crops.

Entomologists work in laboratories and out in nature (fieldwork). They identify new species and uncover evolutionary relationships between species. They help ensure safe and sustainable food production; help us fight plant, animal, and human diseases; work to prevent pest damage to homes, landscapes, and the environment; and many other useful things. They even help conserve rare and endangered species.

But you don't have to have a college degree to enjoy or study insects. Anyone can learn about and enjoy insects, and even collect valuable scientific information or make new discoveries. Today, there are also many opportunities for citizen scientists—members of the general public who help collect and analyze data—to contribute. No matter if you're interested in butterflies, ants, ladybugs, bees, or even earthworms, there are a great many citizen science programs available, and kids can participate in many cases too!

Of course, the first step is probably just exploring and getting to know the many different types of bugs that are right outside your front door.

Butterflies, like this Tiger Swallowtail, are a perennial favorite with all ages.

AN INSECT'S BODY

All insects share several common features. Unlike humans, other mammals, birds, reptiles, and amphibians, insects lack an internal skeleton. Instead, they have

Japanese Beetle

a hard (or generally hard) outer covering called an **exoskeleton**. It serves several functions including protection and support. Like armor, it helps guard the insect's body from damage and water loss (**desiccation**). The exoskeleton also provides support for muscle attachments, which helps bugs move.

The invasive Japanese beetle provides a good example of an insect's hard exoskeleton.

An insect's body is divided into three main sections: the **head, thorax,** and **abdomen.** An insect's head helps the insect sense the world around it; it has two **compound eyes,** two segmented antennae, and mouthparts. The round, and often large, compound

An extreme close-up of a hoverfly's eye

eyes are made up of hundreds of tiny individual lenses. Working together, they provide a single, somewhat grainy (or pixelated) image and gives insects rather good vision, especially for both distance and motion. Above the eyes are two segmented **antennae.** They contain sensory structures that help with smell, taste, touch, and orientation.

A look at a carpenter ant's antennae

Mouthparts are located on the front of the head. The type of mouthparts vary tremendously between different insect groups. Grasshoppers, beetles, and moth and butterfly caterpillars have hardened **mandibles** (jaws) designed for chewing. Others, such as aphids, fleas and mosquitos, have piercing-sucking mouthparts that are a little like straws and used to feed on fluids. There are many other options across insects, including

Close-up of a house fly's mouth

mouthparts designed for sponging (flies), rasping-sucking (thrips, mites, and biting flies), and siphoning (butterflies and moths). Some insects even have highly

reduced, nonfunctional (vestigial) mouthparts or may lack them all together. This is typically the case in one particular life stage, often the adult stage.

A White-Lined Sphinx Moth and its long tongue

As a result, some adult insects don't eat at all, but instead live off the energy reserves they've acquired in an earlier life stage.

A close-up look at an ant

The jaws of a tiger beetle

The **thorax** is an insect's second body section. It supports structures that enable insects to move. All insects have three pairs of jointed legs, one pair on each segment. Legs may be used for running, crawling, jumping, grasping, or capturing prey. Many insects also have one or two pairs of wings. Wings

Ladybugs have four wings.

help insects fly, but they can also be used for other things, such as thermoregulation (temperature control), attracting mates, species recognition, sound production, camouflage, mimicry, and self-defense.

The last and usually the longest or largest section of an insect's body is the **abdomen.** It contains the reproductive, digestive, and excretory systems along with a series of small holes along the sides, called **spiracles,** which insects use to breathe. (Spiracles can also be found on the thorax.) In female

Spiracles viewed up close on a beetle

The stinger of a bumblebee

insects, the tip of the abdomen may have an added structure called an ovipositor, which is used to lay eggs. In some insects, such as bees, wasps, and some ants, the ovipositor

is modified into a stinger that can be used for self-defense or to capture prey.

egg

larva (caterpillar)

pupa (chrysalis)

adult

Butterflies undergo complete metamorphosis.

INSECT DEVELOPMENT

All insects pass through a series of stages as they
grow. This transition is known as **metamorphosis.**
Many insects, such as butterflies, moths, flies, beetles,
bees, and wasps, undergo complete metamorphosis, consisting of four developmental stages: egg,
larva, pupa, and adult. The immature stages look
very different than the adults, eat entirely different
foods, and often live in separate environments. A
good example of this is the life cycle of a butterfly.
Caterpillars are worm-like in appearance, have hard,
chewing mandibles (jaws) perfect for eating plants,
can only crawl, and are typically found on plants.
In comparison, adult butterflies have two large

compound eyes, two antennae, and four large wings. They can fly and easily move from one location to another, as well as feed on liquid flower nectar with a long, tubular mouthpart, called a **proboscis.**

Other insect groups, such as grasshoppers, drag-onflies and damselflies, true bugs, cockroaches, and praying mantises, undergo **incomplete metamor-phosis.** This developmental process has three stages: egg, nymph, and adult. The nymphs often closely resemble the adults in appearance, although they are smaller in size. They also typically share the same food resources and environment that adults do, and they often behave similarly. True bugs are a good example. The nymphs look like smaller versions of the adults.

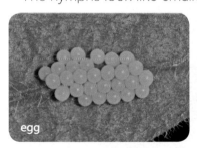

Incomplete metamorphosis.

They have the same piercing-sucking mouthparts, feed on liquid food such as plant sap, live primarily on plants, and typically move by walking. The adults are somewhat larger, can reproduce, and have wings that enable flight.

A house fly feeding on fruit

WHAT INSECTS EAT

Insects feed on a wide range of different foods. Many are **herbivores** and feed on plants. Most are highly specialized and consume specific plant parts, such as leaves, flowers, flower buds, seeds, or developing fruit. Some feed on plant roots, burrow into stems, suck plant sap, or feed on flower nectar or pollen. Other insects are **predators.** They primarily feed on other insects and arthropods. Most are generalists, actively hunting for a variety of available organisms or sitting and waiting for prey to come close. Still others are **scavengers.** They typically feed on

A beetle eating a leaf

dead plant or animal material or animal waste. Most are highly beneficial decomposers that help break down and recycle nutrients. Some insects, such as fleas, are **parasites.** They live on the bodies of other live organisms and feed on their blood. Some insects are **parasitoids.** Most of these are highly specialized flies or wasps. Their developing larvae feed inside or attached to the body of other organisms, primarily insects and arthropods, eventually killing them.

A damselfy eating its prey

WHY INSECTS ARE SMALL

Can you image a dragonfly the size of a large bird? Well, there really were insects that big in prehistoric times, some 300 million years ago. So why are insects so small today? This has been a puzzling question for scientists. One of the most likely answers is related to breathing. Insects breathe through small holes on the outside of their body, called spiracles. These in turn are attached to a complex network of small tubes, called tracheae, which help transport oxygen directly to the insect's body. This system works well for small organisms but becomes much less efficient as body size increases and is limited by the amount of available oxygen in the atmosphere. Hundreds of millions of year ago, oxygen levels were much higher than today, enabling insects to grow much larger.

Honeybees are especially important pollinators for farm crops.

WHY INSECTS ARE IMPORTANT

Insects get a bad rap. They are often considered undesirable, harmful, scary, unclean, or otherwise gross. The real truth is that insects are essential to the health and function of the natural world and our own wellbeing. They are an important food source for many other organisms, including mammals, birds, reptiles, amphibians, other arthropods, and even humans. They help pollinate over 85 percent of all flowering plants on the planet. This includes numerous food crops, such as almonds, blueberries, apples, and even chocolate. In other words, insects are responsible for much of the food that we eat and enjoy every day. Beyond the food humans depend on, the fruits, nuts, and seeds produced by plants provide food for countless other organisms and ensures that plants can reproduce.

Still other insects are **decomposers,** feeding on dead animal and plant material and animal waste. Such insects are nature's recycling crew, helping break down organic matter. In the process, valuable nutrients are recycled back into the soil, water and air. These help plants grow and provides important resources for other organisms.

Many insects are predators. They feed on a wide range of other small creatures, primarily other insects and arthropods. By doing so, they help control garden, agricultural, forest, or other pests such as mosquitoes that may transmit diseases to people or are often considered a nuisance.

Insects also help scientists make important discoveries. Many have been well studied and are considered model organisms for medical, biological, or environmental research. These are organisms used to help better understand how nature works. Fruit flies, for example, have been used to increase our knowledge of genetics, behavior, and human diseases.

Insects also serve as indicators of environmental health or change. The presence or absence of many aquatic insects, such as mayflies, can be used to estimate the level of pollution in streams and rivers. Butterflies and moths are often used to help us understand the effects of habitat loss, pollution, pesticide use, or a changing climate.

Types of Bugs

While this book focuses mostly on insects, we have also included a few other arthropods. Arthropods belong to the phylum Arthropoda and represent the largest and most successful group of organisms in the animal kingdom. They include insects, spiders, millipedes, centipedes and crustaceans, and can be divided into more than 30 different subgroups called orders. The members of each have certain basic characteristics and behaviors that can be particularly

Pillbug

useful for iden-tification. The following include some of the most interesting, distinctive, and commonly found orders covered in this book. Insects, are included in the book first, followed by familiar arthropods, such as spiders, centipedes, and millipedes, which are arthropods, but not insects.

BUTTERFLIES AND MOTHS (ORDER LEPIDOPTERA)

Butterflies and moths are probably one of the most familiar insect groups. The adults are often large, brightly colored, and pretty easy to spot. They have two pairs of transparent wings that are covered with numerous tiny scales that determine their color and pattern. They have two large compound eyes, two elongated segmented antennae, and straw-like mouthparts (although in some species they are highly reduced or nonfunctioning) that help them feed on various fluids such as flower nectar. Butterflies are active during the day. While most moths fly only at night, there are some that can be seen during the day or at dusk and dawn. Many actively visit flowers and are important pollinators. Butterflies and moths undergo a complete metamorphosis, developing through four stages: egg, larva (or caterpillar), pupa, and adult. The larvae, known as caterpillars, are primarily plant feeders and have chewing mouthparts.

BEES, WASPS, AND ANTS (ORDER HYMENOPTERA)

This is a large and diverse group of insects. Many species have complex social systems that include elaborate nests and a division of labor, with groups of individuals (**castes**) having specific jobs that benefit the entire colony. Adults typically have two pairs of transparent wings (although some species or individuals don't have wings), and two large compound eyes. Wasps and ants have chewing mouthparts, and bees have a tongue for feeding on liquids such as flower nectar. The majority of adults also have a narrow waist between the thorax and abdomen.

Many adult bees and wasps feed on nectar and/or pollen. These tend to be common flower visitors and beneficial pollinators. Most ants, however, are predators or scavengers, feeding on a wide range of available food. All bees, wasps, and ants undergo a complete metamorphosis, developing through four stages: egg, larva, pupa, and adult. The larvae feed on a variety of resources including pollen, nectar, plant material, and even other insects. In many cases, this food is initially provided by adults or in a social colony. Some species may also be parasitoids on other insects or arthropods. Many bees, wasps, and ants can sting or bite, particularly if threatened.

TRUE BUGS (ORDER HEMIPTERA)

This is another large and diverse insect group. They vary considerably in their size, appearance and behavior. Adults have two pairs of wings, the first pair being partially thickened at the base. Their wings fold over the back of the insect's body, often resulting in a distinctive X shaped pattern. True bugs have piercing-sucking mouthparts. Many feed on plant juices while others are predatory and feed on other small organisms. True bugs undergo incomplete metamorphosis, developing through three stages: egg, nymph, and adult. The nymphs often closely resemble the adults in appearance. Most true bugs live on land and on vegetation although a few groups are aquatic and occur in freshwater habitats.

BEETLES (ORDER COLEOPTERA)

Beetles are incredibly diverse. With nearly 400,000 different species, they represent about 40 percent of all known insects. The adults tend to be rather large, full-bodied, and somewhat round or oval in shape. They have two pairs of wings. The first one is modified into hard, often shiny protective covers called elytra. These cover the two larger wings beneath that are used to fly. Beetles occur both in terrestrial (land) and aquatic (water) environments. They have chewing mouthparts with hardened mandibles (jaws) that are adapted for chewing. Some feed as predators on other small invertebrates, while others are herbivores and eat plant parts. Still others are scavengers on animal waste or dead plant or animal material. Beetles undergo complete metamorphosis, developing through four stages: egg, larva, pupa, and adult. Beetles may be active during the day or at night, and many are attracted to artificial lights.

FLIES (ORDER DIPTERA)

Flies are a diverse group of insects that are often (unfairly!) considered unattractive or a nuisance. Adults have compact bodies, large compound eyes, short antennae, and one pair of transparent wings. The second pair of wings (rear wings) is modified into small, club-like structures, called halteres. These help stabilize the fly during flight. Adults may have one of several types of mouthparts; some are adapted for piercing, sucking, or sponging up liquid foods. Flies undergo a complete metamorphosis, developing through four stages: egg, larva, pupa, and adult. The larvae, called maggots, lack legs and live in a variety of different habitats, including on land and in the water where they feed on decaying plant or animal material or are predators of other animals. Many adults regularly visit flowers and are important pollinators. A small number of species are parasitoids on other insects.

DRAGONFLIES AND DAMSELFLIES (ORDER ODONATA)

This is a relatively small group that includes somewhat prehistoric-looking insects. Adults have large rounded heads, two large compound eyes, long, slender abdomens, and two pairs of elongated transparent wings with numerous veins. The adults are active during the day and are often brightly colored. They are predators with chewing mouthparts and use their long, spiny legs to capture prey in flight. Dragonflies and damselflies undergo incomplete metamorphosis, developing through three stages: egg, nymph, and adult. The nymphs, called naiads, live in freshwater habitats. They prey on various smaller insects and other aquatic organisms.

GRASSHOPPERS, CRICKETS, KATYDIDS, AND OTHERS (ORDER ORTHOPTERA)

Most members of this group are large, stout insects that are found on land. The have two relatively large compound eyes, antennae that are often long, and two pairs of wings. The first pair of wings is narrow, thick, and somewhat hardened and covers a second larger set of wings. Both pairs of wings are held over the back while the insect is at rest. In many species, the wings are not used for flight but are used to produce sound in order to attract mates. The hind legs are enlarged and used for jumping. Grasshoppers, crickets, and katydids undergo incomplete metamorphosis, developing through three stages: egg, nymph, and adult. The young nymphs closely resemble the adults in appearance. Both adults and nymphs have chewing mouthparts and mostly feed on plant material.

COCKROACHES AND TERMITES (ORDER BLATTODEA)

This is a small and ancient group of insects. Cock-roaches have a somewhat flattened oval body, very long antennae, and two pairs of membranous wings. Some species are considered household pests. They have chewing mouthparts and feed on a variety of dead animal and plant material, including food scraps. They are generally active at night and hide in dark moist locations during the day. Termites are social insects much like wasps, ants and bees, and they have larger colonies. They have chewing mouthparts feed on dead plant material including wood. As a result, some species can cause serious damage to homes or other structures. Both cockroaches and termites undergo an incomplete metamorphosis, developing through three stages: egg, nymph, and adult.

ANTLIONS AND LACEWINGS (ORDER NEUROPTERA)

These tend to be somewhat small, delicate-looking
insects that have slender, elongated bodies and two
pairs of transparent wings with numerous fine veins.
The predatory adults have chewing mouthparts and
feed on other insects. The larvae are also predators that actively hunt, trap, or sit and wait for prey.
They have modified jaw-like mouthparts to capture
prey and suck out the internal fluids. They undergo
a complete metamorphosis, developing through four
stages: egg, larva, pupa, and adult. They tend to be
very weak fliers and are often attracted to artificial
lights at night.

EARWIGS (ORDER DERMAPTERA)

Earwigs are small and somewhat unique-looking insects. They have somewhat flattened, elongated bodies, long antennae, and two pairs of short leathery wings. On their rear end, they have a noticeable pair of pincer-like features called cerci. They undergo incomplete metamorphosis, developing through three stages: egg, nymph and adult. They are primarily active at night and hide in dark moist locations during the day. They have chewing mouthparts and tend to be scavengers, feeding on a variety of living and dead plant and animal material.

 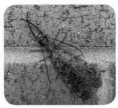 

ALDERFLIES, DOBSONFLIES, AND FISHFLIES (ORDER MEGALOPTERA)

These tend to be rather large, somewhat prehistoric-looking insects. They have elongated, soft bodies with long antennae, chewing mouthparts, and two pairs of large, heavily veined wings. They are generally weak and somewhat clumsy fliers. They undergo incomplete metamorphosis, developing through three stages: egg, nymph, and adult. While the adults live on land, immature individuals are found in freshwater aquatic habitats, such as streams and rivers. Many adults are short lived and are attracted to artificial lights at night.

MANTISES (ORDER MANTODEA)

Praying mantises are large and unique insects. They have elongated bodies with a distinctive triangular head, large compound eyes, and two pairs of membranous wings. Their front legs are enlarged, bear numerous spines and are designed for tightly grasping prey. They undergo incomplete metamorphosis, developing through three stages: egg, nymph, and adult. Both the nymphs and adults are camouflaged and blend into vegetation. They are sit-and-wait predators and have chewing mouthparts. Praying mantises typically have one generation per year. Adults are sometimes attracted to artificial lights at night.

WALKING STICKS (ORDER PHASMIDA)

As their name suggests, walking sticks tend to resemble a small twig or branch. They are relatively large insects with long, slender bodies, legs and antennae. They move very slowly, have chewing mouthparts, and feed on plants. They undergo incomplete metamorphosis, developing through three stages: egg, nymph, and adult. Only a small number of species occur in the United States.

How and Where to Find Bugs

North America is a wonderful place to learn about bugs. While some insects require specialized environments and may be limited to a particular region or even just a few specific locations, many are common and can be found right in your own yard, a neighboring field, or nearby park or natural area. In fact, no matter where you live, there are a great many insects around to find. However, due to their small size and often secretive behaviors, they can be easy to miss unless you know where to look. Observing and studying insects is fun and relatively easy. It's like going on a miniature safari. Instead of lions, elephants, and giraffes, you'll quickly discover a small, hidden world full of weird and amazing creatures, bizarre behaviors, and really cool interactions.

Of course, insects and other arthropods occupy an amazing variety of ecological **niches**—a niche is the individual role and position an organism occupies in an ecosystem. Even a small space in your yard such as a blooming plant or a log on the ground can support an amazing variety of species and offer hours of exciting exploration. The following provides a brief overview of some of the best places to start your adventure.

BEWARE OF BITES, STINGS, AND OTHER HAZARDS

Before you go out looking for bugs, be aware that some of the animals described in this book can bite, sting, or pinch. So when you're out bug hunting, go with an adult. Be sure to wear gloves and use caution when turning over logs or other objects, or when reaching into places you can't see inside of.

Bites or stings usually just cause temporary pain, redness, itching, or minor swelling, and these injuries usually heal on their own. Wearing gloves, keeping a distance, and simply avoid handling the bugs at all helps prevents nearly all bites. With that said, if you're allergic to a specific kind of insect bite or sting bees, wasps, and ants are among the most common culprits—a bite or a sting can be very serious and can have life-threatening symptoms that require emergency treatment. If you know you're allergic, or someone in your family is, don't closely approach, bother, or handle insects, and always be aware of your surroundings. Also be aware of other potentially dangerous critters (like snakes and scorpions) in your area and how to avoid them.

Of course, the weather and the sun pose a much greater risk than most bugs, so dress appropriately and take necessary precautions. Protect yourself from the sun and heat by wearing sunscreen, a hat, loose fitting clothes, and carry plenty of water. Avoid going outside during the hottest time of the day. In fact, many insects also avoid this time and tend to be less active. When possible, wear long pants and sturdy shoes. Apply insect repellent to protect yourself against mosquitoes, ticks, and chiggers. Lastly, be aware of the weather. Pop-up thunderstorms can be common in many places. Such storms can produce heavy rain and lightning. If you hear thunder, quickly head back inside. A little planning will ensure that your expedition is safe and fun.

ON OR UNDER LOGS

Logs provide great habitat and resources for many insects and other arthropods. In many ways, they are a rich, miniature ecosystem alive with critters of all kinds. Bugs may live on, in, or under the slowly decaying wood, so you have to look very closely to see any signs of life. In general, these organisms come in one of four different categories: decomposers, predators, nesters, and hiders.

Decomposers are organisms that feed on decaying material. In the process, they help break down the nutrients and enable them to be recycled back into the environment for other plants or animals to use. Decomposers may be found under the log, under loose bark on the log, or even in the decaying wood of the log itself. Some common examples include pillbugs, beetle grubs, snails, slugs, and even earthworms.

The next group of insects that use a decaying log are nesters. Like miniature developers and architects, they tunnel through the decaying wood as well as the soil underneath, creating a maze of tunnels and chambers for their developing colony. Both termites and many ant species are nesters that inhabit dead wood. In the process, they help break down the log over time and create additional tunnels, cavities, and food for other organisms to use.

Logs also provide shelter to many organisms. Many insects and other arthropods are active at night. During the day, they often seek the protection in moist, dark, and cool locations—perfect hiding places to avoid the heat of the day or detection by potential predators. In addition to temporary shelters, logs often offer ideal sites for hibernating organisms. Many wasps, bees, millipedes, lady beetles, leafhoppers, and others survive the cooler winter months when conditions for continued development is not ideal in such protected sites. You may even a silken cocoon or two of various moths on or around a fallen log.

The abundance of organisms found in, on, and around logs attracts a variety of predators. They seek to take advantage of the variety of available prey. While some may call the log home, others are just passing by as they actively hunt in the surrounding environment. Some examples of predators include earwigs, centipedes, ground beetles, and wolf spiders.

HOW TO HUNT FOR BUGS ON OR UNDER LOGS

So now you know what kind of insects to look for on or under logs, it's time to start looking. It may be useful to have a magnifying glass and a wide-mouth plastic jar with a lid before heading outside. An old plastic peanut butter or mayonnaise jar is ideal. Once you find a log, take a few minutes to look it over carefully. Some organisms worth observing might be on or around the log. Then, carefully roll the log over. Be prepared to look quickly as many organisms will rapidly scurry away when disturbed. Wearing gloves, use the plastic jar to temporarily capture any critters for closer inspection. Examine the underside of the log and the ground beneath for insects, other arthropods, or signs of them (such as tunnels or holes). You want to use the magnifying class to study some of the smaller animals. When you are done looking, always gently return the log to its original position so you don't damage their sheltering site or home. Then move on to the next log and continue the process. You will be amazed at all the critters you'll find!

IN OR UNDER LEAF LITTER OR MULCH

When you walk through your yard, under trees, or in the woods, look down and pay attention to all the fallen leaves on the ground. This layer of old, dead leaves and the associated twigs, discarded flowers, fruit, and shed bark is actually a habitat all its own and

home to a surprising variety of small critters. Just like with logs, it provides food and protected, often cool, moist sites that support decomposers, predators, nesters, and hiders. Earthworms, pill bugs, some fly larvae, snails, slugs, earwigs, and many others feed on dead or decaying plant material and can be common in and under leaf litter. Garden mulch such as pine bark, pine needles, or wood shavings is also great to explore. Like leaf litter, it provides a resource of decaying organic material and many nooks and crannies under which many bugs can hide or live. Additional predators or scavengers found in leaf litter or under mulch include some adult beetles and their larvae, ants, millipedes, cockroaches, centipedes, and earwigs. Many of these are active at night and spend the daylight hours hidden safely under the protective layers. These organisms also nest or reproduce in the same environment. Lastly, leaf litter or mulch also provides numerous snug, sheltered sites for organisms to successfully overwinter.

How to Look for Insects in Leaf Litter

Similar to a dead log, leaf litter or mulch initially looks pretty lifeless until you dig in a bit and look more closely. Once again, it may be useful to have a magnifying glass and a wide-mouth plastic jar with a lid, as well as a small garden trowel and a plastic bowl before you start. Find a spot in your yard or nearby woods and get down and simply watch for a bit. You may see or hear a variety of critters crawling over or in the leaf litter. Then, the small garden trowel and gently start pulling away the layers of leaves and debris, watching closely at what you uncover. The plastic jar can be used to temporarily capture any small organisms for closer inspection. Continue to uncover the debris until you get to the moist, decomposed organic material and soil beneath. This will naturally look darker in color and often be more of a matted material. Using the trowel, now slowly dig down, taking a few small scoops and place them in the bowl. This will allow you to inspect that material in greater detail to see what's found inside. You can do the same with mulch. When finished, return the organic material and soil to the same location and be sure to release any captured critters. You may wish to also explore at night and simply observe the ground to see a wider array of active animals. For this it is helpful to have a small flashlight or headlamp. And remember; if heading outside after dark, always tell an adult or bring one with you.

BENEATH TREE BARK

Dead trees, stumps and decaying logs are often covered with loosening bark. While many insects and other arthropods live in or under dead or decaying wood, some, or at least evidence of their current or past presence, can also be found under bark. Be very careful around dead trees or large stumps, as they are often unstable or can sometimes be home to other critters (such as snakes). Always explore such places with an adult for safety.

How to Find Insects Under Tree Bark

Once a safe tree, stump, or log has been located, start by observing the exterior for signs of life. Do you see any small holes or other signs of activity? Then, slowly and carefully remove pieces of loose bark to see what lies beneath. Look quickly, as many insects will quickly scuttle away from the disturbance. A wide-mouth jar is again handy, as it enables you to examine your finds. You may also want to have a large flat-head screwdriver. This will help to carefully dislodge pieces of bark without using your fingers. Once the bark is removed, explore both the uncovered dead wood and the back of the bark as you may find organisms on both. Some common organisms that you may encounter include ants and their eggs/pupas, centipedes, pill bugs, small beetles, beetle grubs, and earwigs, among many others. If you explore these sites in fall and winter, you may also discover a few hibernating insects.

Beyond any living critters, you will likely also see some evidence of their activity, past or present. This may include everything from small holes and chambers to a network of small tunnels and routes that were created by from bark beetles or other wood-boring insects. The resulting network of designs can be quite extensive and appear almost like a piece of artwork. Use the magnifying glass to examine the surface in greater detail. Dead trees and larger stumps will continue to decay. As they do, many new organisms may continue to colonize them. So, once a good site is located, continue to follow it over time.

ON THE GROUND OR UNDER OTHER OBJECTS

Besides logs, leaf litter or mulch, there are many other objects on the ground worth investigating. Rocks, old boards, landscape pavers, and even flower pots are great places under which insects may hide or live. As you explore, gently turn over the objects.

You're likely to spot earthworms, earwigs, pill bugs, millipedes, centipedes, snails, cockroaches, and various other critters. Once you're finished looking, gently return the object to its original position before moving on.

On the Ground
Numerous insects and arthropods live on the ground, and they spend all or some of their time foraging, nesting or otherwise scurrying along the ground in either natural or artificial areas. How many insects—and how many different kinds you find—depends greatly on the type of environment, the season, and the level of disturbance present. For example, the organisms found directly around your home and yard are often different than those found in a nearby woods or meadows. Nonetheless, in pretty much any area, there are a number of interesting ground-dwelling critters to discover. Several, such as wolf spiders, beetles, and ants are active hunters and move about in search of available prey. Many others are considered scavengers, feeding on a variety of living and dead animal or plant material. These include various ants, earwigs, centipedes, millipedes, snails, slugs, pill bugs, and others. As a large number

of these may be most active at night, try exploring places around your home and yard after dark. Take a flashlight or wear a head lamp for best results. You'll be amazed at what you can find. And remember, if heading outside at night, have an adult tag along.

Various insects and other arthropods also nest in the soil. This includes many native bees and wasps, for example. In turn, some wasps and bee flies search out and parasitize these nests. Red imported fire ants (primarily found in the eastern and southern United States) and many other ants species are ground nesters. They create extensive underground colonies and actively forage for food in the surrounding area. Mole crickets spend most of their lives underground and create nest chambers to lay their eggs. The larvae of rainbow scarabs  and green June beetles also live and feed underground, as do cicada nymphs. Other insects, such as southern field crickets, are scavengers and are most often encountered scurrying across the ground.

Some insects also feed at or near ground level. Millipedes and field crickets are scavengers and regularly scurry across the ground in search of food. Male butterflies regularly visit wet sand, gravel, mud puddles, or animal dung (poop) to gain nutrients. Many butterfly and moth larvae will periodically be seen wandering along the ground. When you see them doing that, they've finished feeding and are searching for suitable and protected places to pupate (spin a cocoon or transform into a chrysalis). In some cases, the larvae of various insects, including those of some very beautiful moth varieties actually pupae in the soil. While it may not be the first place you think of to look for insects and other arthropods, the ground is actually a habitat bustling with life of all kinds. Spend some time looking down and see what you can find.

ON PLANTS

Plants provide a variety of important resources for insects—everything from food to shelter. A large percentage of insects and other arthropods are herbivores (plant feeders). They feed on or in nearly every plant part, from stems, sap, and leaves to roots, flower buds, and fruit. Those that feed on leaves are often the most familiar as they often create visible feeding damage as they nibble away. However, adult and immature insects often feed on very different foods. Butterflies and moths are good examples. As caterpillars, they readily munch on leaves and other plant parts; as adults, they feed only on liquid foods, such as flower nectar, tree sap, or the juices from fermenting fruit. Many caterpillars are specialists and can only feed on a small number of different plants. By contrast, grasshoppers, katydids, and walking sticks tend to be more generalist herbivores, capable of nibbling away on the leaves of a wide variety of plant species. The mouthparts of many plant feeding insects are designed for chewing. They have hard mandibles perfect for cutting through leaves and other plant parts. Many others have piercing-sucking mouthparts that are used to pierce plant tissues and suck out sap.

The abundance of plant feeders also attracts many predators ready to find a hearty meal. These include active hunters, such as paper wasps, green lynx spiders, lady beetles, and spined soldier bugs, to various sit-and-wait predators. Praying mantises are a perfect example. Armed with good vision, a well-camouflaged body, and powerful front legs to capture and hold prey, they await unsuspecting insects that come too close.

How to Look for Insects on Plants

Carefully inspecting plants will reveal all sorts of unusual critters. Look for signs of feeding. This is a good place to start, and be sure to inspect all areas of the plant, not just the leaves. You can also put down a white sheet or a cloth beneath overhanging branches or taller plants and beat the vegetation with a stick. This will knock off many insects onto the sheet below where they can be more closely observed.

You can also use an insect net to vigorously sweep through grasses and other vegetation and then look inside to see what critters have been dislodged. Once spotted, use the large-mouth plastic jar to temporarily capture what you find. A magnifying glass is also handy as many of the critters may be quite small. And remember to release any organisms you capture once you are done exploring.

ON FLOWERS

Many insects are attracted to flowers. They provide abundant food in the form of sugary nectar and protein-rich pollen for insects such as bees, butterflies, moths, and wasps. In return, the insects help pollinate the flowers. Sometimes, you may also find various herbivores on flowers.

Grasshoppers, aphids, various beetles and true bugs, and even caterpillars may feed on flowers, flower buds or developing fruit or seeds. You'll also likely run into numerous predators such as green lynx spiders, lady beetles, robber flies, and praying mantises. Just like at a buffet, they take advantage of the numerous and varied flower visitors.

Looking for Insects on Flowers

While single flowers attract insects, it's often best to look for a larger patch of many blooming plants. Once found, stand back and observe for a few minutes before getting too close. If the flowers are attracting insects, you should notice a fair amount of insects coming and going. Particularly noticeable insects include bees, wasps, butterflies, and day-flying moths. As you look more closely, you may notice a variety of smaller and less obvious critters, such as beetles and flies. The vast majority of these insects are attracted to nectar and pollen, and they are generally classified as pollinators. As you start looking, you will quickly notice that different flowers attract different organisms and that some species, types, and colors of flowers are much more attractive than others. Planting a flower garden in your yard, on a balcony, or at your school is a great way to help provide food and habitat for many of these beneficial organisms and an easy way to bring bugs to you, making observation easy. Even a small container garden is beneficial, and can be easily altered or moved around as needed. (See page 119 for tips on how to build your own container garden.)

AT LIGHTS

Artificial lights are a magnet for insects that are active at night. They are drawn in from the darkness and often linger until dawn near the light. Scientists aren't exactly sure why bugs are attracted to artificial lights. It may be that the light interferes with their natural navigational cues (such as the moon). It may also be due to the wavelengths that a particular light emits, as we know insects are more attracted to ultraviolet (UV) and short wavelength colors. Parking lots, gas stations, or even the lights around your home or apartment are a great place to start looking. You can also put out your own light in front of a hanging white sheet (see page 110). While special lights called black lights are often best, a plain incandescent or florescent bulb will is a perfect start. Warm, cloudy, or moonless nights are often the best, as more insects tend to be active on darker nights. If your parents or another adult family member is willing, drive out to the country away from any light pollution for the best results. Regardless of where you go, artificial lights are a surefire way to draw in a wide variety of bugs. Just be sure to make sure you wear dark-colored clothes so the bugs don't mistake you for the lit-up sheet.

How to Find Insects at a Light

On a good night, a productive light can attract a huge number and variety of animals. Even from a distance you can spot larger insects circling about or perched an adjacent structure or wall. Have a large-mouth plastic jar and a flashlight or headlamp handy. Moths are often the most numerous and obvious. They range greatly in size, from giant silkworm moths

such as the Luna Moth or Polyphemus Moth to very tiny, but beautiful ones, which deserve a much closer look. katydids, giant water bugs, cockroaches, green lacewings, antlions, and various beetles are regular visitors too. Beyond insects, lights often also attract some predators. Spiders often build webs near light sources to take full advantage of the abundant and easily accessible prey. Keep in mind that the insects that come to lights vary throughout the year. What you see in early spring is often different than later in the summer or fall. In some parts of the country, lights might not attract much once winter sets in, but further south, you might find insects all year long. And remember, if heading outside after dark, always let an adult know and/or have them join you.

IN OR NEAR WATER

Various insects live in or around water for some portion of their life cycle. Freshwater streams, ponds, rivers, and even lakes can provide ideal habitat and access to food resources. Even small ponds or a water feature in your yard may attract insects.

Looking for Insects in Water

As you approach a stream or pond, move slowly and carefully watch for any activity around the edges of the water and nearby vegetation. Dragonflies and damselflies are common and conspicuous in such areas. They actively fly around the habitat, often scurrying low over the water to lay eggs, hunt for small flying insects, or perch on vegetation or bare branches that have fallen in the water. Pause briefly near the water and watch the activity. It can be quite amazing! Next, scan the surface of the water for motion. You may see insects scurrying on the surface of the water or ripples indicating activity bellow. In shallow water or around a pond margins you may also see dragonfly or damselfly naiads (immature dragonflies) on submerged vegetation or on the silty bottom. A small aquatic or aquarium net can be used to explore this world. In many ways, this aquatic environment is truly a hidden world of excitement and discovery.

Of course, be very careful around water. Often objects and even the edges of ponds may be slippery or unstable. Near deep water, wear a life jacket and avoid walking into vegetation, especially near wetlands, and only do so with a parent or adult present.

Water boatman (see page 80)

Common Insects and Bugs

BLACK SWALLOWTAIL

Size: Large; wingspan of 3.25–4.2 inches

Where You'll See It: Throughout much of the eastern half of the US, southwestern US, and southeastern Canada

What It Looks Like: Mostly black; male has a wide central yellow band of spots; female has less of a yellow spot band but more blue on hind wings.

One of the most common garden butterflies in the eastern US. Adults are strong fliers; adult butterflies look like (mimic) the toxic Pipevine Swallowtail, which helps prevent them from getting eaten by predators.

Caterpillars are green with black bands that have yellow-orange spots. When disturbed, caterpillars push out an orange, forked, horn-like structure called an **osmeterium.** It is stinky and has chemicals that bother predators.

EASTERN TIGER SWALLOWTAIL

Size: Large; wingspan of 3.5–6.0 inches

Where You'll See It: Throughout most of the eastern US and southeastern Canada

What It Looks Like: A yellow-and-black butterfly with yellow wings with black stripes; hind wing has a single tail.

Adults are strong, fast fliers and fly up into the trees; they are very fond of flowers and feed with their wings open. Males often puddle at wet ground.

Males are always yellow with black stripes; females may look like males or be mostly black. Females have more blue on the upper side of the hind wings. When mostly black, the females are mimicking the toxic Pipevine Swallowtail, which provides protection from predators.

CABBAGE WHITE
Size: Medium; wingspan of 1.5–2.0 inches

Where You'll See It: Throughout the US and southern Canada; at flowers

What It Looks Like: Mostly white, with black wing tips on the front wings; black spots on wings.

Easy to spot in almost any open area, including home vegetable gardens or farm fields. Adults are slow and somewhat clumsy when flying; they feed and rest with their wings closed or partially open.

Accidentally introduced to the US from Europe in 1860, the Cabbage White (also known as the European Cabbage Butterfly) is one of the few butterfly species that is a serious agricultural and garden pest, damaging crops and garden plants, such as cabbage and broccoli.

CLOUDLESS SULPHUR
Size: Large; wingspan of 2.2–3.25 inches

Where You'll See It: Most common in the eastern and southern US, it's occasionally seen in the northern US too

What It Looks Like: Large; male has bright yellow wings; female has some darker markings.

Adults fly quickly; they like to visit flowers; they eat and rest with their wings closed; they have a very long proboscis (a tongue-like mouthpart) that helps it feed at many long tubular blossoms.

Seen in open, sunny areas, including yards, gardens, parks, roadsides, and fields. Males often group together at wet ground; this is called puddling. Adults migrate southward in the fall.

AMERICAN COPPER

Size: Small; wingspan of 0.9–1.4 inches

Where You'll See It: Northern two-thirds of US, parts of the Mountain West, and southeastern Canada

What It Looks Like: Small; bright reddish-orange front wings with scattered black spots and gray back wings with a wide scalloped orange border.

The bright reddish-orange adults often perch on low plants or bare soil with their wings held in a partially open position. They fly weakly and are easy to watch up-close when they're feeding. Sometimes, you can spot dozens or hundreds of them in one place. When you first see one in bright sunlight, you'll see why this butterfly is called a copper.

Although it's called the American Copper, some scientists think that some populations might have been unintentionally introduced from Europe!

GRAY HAIRSTREAK

Size: Small; wingspan of 1.0–1.5 inches

Where You'll See It: Throughout the US and southern Canada

What It Looks Like: wings above are dark gray; wings below are light gray with a narrow black line through the center; hind wing has a reddish-orange hind wing patch on both sides near a single, hair-like tail.

This is one of the most common and widespread hairstreak butterflies, but it's rarely seen in large numbers when found. These hairstreaks generally feed and rest with their wings closed but occasionally partially open, which is unusual for most hairstreaks.

Its caterpillars are variable in color from green to pink with short hairs and have an overall slug-like shape; they feed on the flowers and fruit of a huge variety of different plants.

GREAT PURPLE HAIRSTREAK
Size: Small; wingspan of 1.0–1.5 inches

Where You'll See It: Throughout the southern half of the US; found in yards, parks, and gardens

What It Looks Like: Males are black with bright blue on the wings above; females have less blue; on both males and females, the underside of the back wing is black with two obvious hair-like tails located near metallic green-and-blue spots; the abdomen is reddish-orange.

This is one of the largest hairstreak butterflies in the US; its bright colors warn predators that it tastes bad. The tails look like antennae, helping fool predators into attacking the wings (not its head). Adults spend most of their time high in the trees; they regularly come down to flowers and feed and rest with their wings closed. Caterpillars feed on mistletoe.

EASTERN TAILED BLUE
Size: Small; wingspan of 0.75–1 inch

Where You'll See It: Throughout much of the US and southeastern Canada

What It Looks Like: Male are bright blue with a narrow brown border; female is brown above; both have one or two small orange back wing spots and a single, hair-like tail at the bottom of both wings.

This small butterfly is named for its distinctive tails on its hind wings. Adults love flowers and are easily attracted to gardens. Unlike other hairstreaks or blue butterflies, it often perches with its wings open. Males often gather in small "puddle clubs" at damp sand or gravel.

Its thin tails resemble antennae and help deflect the attack of predators, such as jumping spiders, away from the insect's body.

GULF FRITILLARY

Size: Large; wingspan of 2.5–3.0 inches

Where You'll See It: Throughout the southern half of the US

What It Looks Like: Large; orange elongated wings with back markings; hind wing below brown with elongated silvery spots.

Adults have a swift, somewhat low flight; they like flowers and are found in gardens. One of the most abundant and frequently encountered garden butterflies in the southern US; look for its elongated wings and silvery hind wing spots to tell it apart from the somewhat similar-looking Monarch.

Like the Monarch, the Gulf Fritillary migrates southward in fall. The caterpillars are orange with greenish-black stripes and black, branched spines.

MONARCH

Size: Large; wingspan of 3.5–4.5 inches

Where You'll See It: Throughout the US and southern Canada

What It Looks Like: Large orange butterfly with black wing veins and white-spotted black wing borders.

The adult Monarch's brilliant orange-and-black wing colors warn predators to stay away. As the caterpillars feed, the chemicals from the plants accumulate in their body, making them and the later adults taste very bad to birds and other predators. The caterpillar is white with yellow-and-black stripes with a pair of long black filaments on each end.

Monarchs are declining and need your help; planting milkweed and other flowers in the garden provides food for the caterpillars and adult butterflies.

Adult Monarchs migrate in fall, with some traveling over 3,000 miles.

COMMON BUCKEYE

Size: Large; wingspan of 1.5–2.5 inches

Where You'll See It: Throughout most of the US and southeastern Canada

What It Looks Like: Brown wings with large eyespots (eye-like spots); front wing with an obvious white patch and two orange bars. The underside of the hindwings are light brown in summer and turn a darker reddish brown in winter.

Adults fly quickly and low to the ground; they often land on the ground or on plants; they leave their wings open or partially open, but they get scared easily and are hard to see up-close.

These butterflies temporarily colonize much of the central and northern US each summer. Unable to survive freezing temperatures, adults migrate south in the fall to spend the winter.

MOURNING CLOAK

Size: Large; wingspan of 3.0–4.0 inches

Where You'll See It: Throughout the US and southern Canada

What It Looks Like: Black wings with a wide irregular yellow border and a row of bright purple-blue spots.

This lovely butterfly has a morbid name but is often the first sign of spring; adults emerge in early summer to breed, then lie dormant until fall. They then feed before seeking sheltered locations to spend the winter in. They are among the longest-lived butterfly species—some adults live over 10 months.

Hibernating adults often fly out on warm winter days, even if there is snow. Adults have a strong, darting flight and are often hard to closely approach.

Caterpillars are spiny and gray and red; they feed in groups on a wide range of trees.

PAINTED LADY

Size: Medium-size; wingspan of 1.75–2.40 inches

Where You'll See It: Throughout the US and southern Canada

What It Looks Like: Pinkish orange wings above with dark markings and white spots near the tip of the front wing; wings below are brown with whitish patches and a cobweb-like pattern.

The adults have a quick, erratic flight, usually close to the ground but they like to stop to perch or visit flowers.

Unable to survive freezing temperatures, the Painted Lady typically overwinters in Mexico and annually recolonizes much of North America each summer. Populations vary year by year; it occasionally has huge population outbreaks.

The dark, spiny caterpillars build shelters of loose webbing on their host plants.

FIERY SKIPPER

Size: Small; wingspan of 1.0–1.25 inches

Where You'll See It: Southern half of the US, often temporarily colonizes the Midwest, Northeast, and southeast-ern Canada each year

What It Looks Like: Male is bright orange with a jagged black border and a black front wing patch; female is dark brown with orange spots; underside of back wing is golden-orange in males or light brown in females with numerous small dark spots; short antennae.

Adults fly low to the ground with a rapid, darting flight but regularly visit flowers or rest on low vegetation; sometimes many adults visit flowers at the same time. They feed and perch with their front wings held partially open and hind wings separated and lowered further.

WHIRLABOUT

Size: Small; wingspan of 1.0–1.25 inches

Where You'll See It: Southeastern US, occasionally farther north

What It Looks Like: Short antennae; male is bright orange with a black border and black patch on the front wing; female is dark brown with whitish spots; underside of the back wing is golden-orange in males (brown in females) with two bands of larger dark spots.

Adults have a quick flight low to the ground, stopping at flowers or to rest on plants; they often feed and perch with their front wings held partially open and hind wings separated and lowered.

Caterpillars are brownish-green with a thin dark brown line, and a round black head.

Often found alongside the Fiery Skipper, both are common in yards; sometimes many will visit flowers at the same time.

LONG-TAILED SKIPPER

Size: Large; wingspan of 1.5–2.0 inches

Where You'll See It: Throughout the southeastern US, sometimes farther north

What It Looks Like: Brown wings with bluish-green on the wing bases and body; hind wing has a long tail; resembles a small swallowtail butterfly.

Adults have a quick, darting flight and regularly visit flowers or perch on plants; they often rest and feed with their wings partially open.

Caterpillars are green with yellow stripes, and have a round, reddish-brown head with two orange spots and a black collar. They construct shelters on host plants by tying leaves together with silk.

SILVER-SPOTTED SKIPPER

Size: Large; wingspan of 1.75–2.4 inches

Where You'll See It: Throughout most of the US and southern Canada

What It Looks Like: Large with a stout body; brown wings with a wide, clear white patch in the center of the hind wing below; no other large skipper has these markings.

Adults are strong fliers but regularly visit flowers for nectar; males may also be found at damp ground, animal dung or bird droppings; males often perch on vegetation and fly out to investigate passing insects.

Caterpillars are yellow with dark stripes and a round, brown head with two orange spots. They build shelters on plants by tying leaves together with silk. They rest in the shelters during the day and come out at night to feed on leaves; they forcibly fling their frass (poop) out of their leaf shelters.

IMPERIAL MOTH

Size: Large; wingspan of 3.5–6.8 inches

Where You'll See It: Eastern US and southeastern Canada

What It Looks Like: somewhat long yellow wings with a varying degree of purplish-brown markings; wings resemble fallen leaves.

One of the largest moths in the US, female Imperial Moths can have a wingspan of over six inches; females are much larger than males. Adults are often attracted to artificial lights, males are seen more often than females.

The caterpillars are either green or brown and are covered with fine hairs and have four short knobby horns behind their head. Some caterpillars can be five inches long when fully grown! Unlike many moths, they pupate in the soil and do not spin a cocoon.

IO MOTH

Size: Medium-size; wingspan of 2.0–3.0 inches

Where You'll See It: Eastern US and southeastern Canada

What It Looks Like: Male with mottled yellow front wings; female with spotted reddish-brown front wings, each hind wing has a single large eyespot.

Adults are nocturnal and commonly attracted to artificial lights; adults don't feed and don't have working mouthparts.

Caterpillars are bright green with red-and-white side stripes and numerous branched spines; they feed in groups and spin papery silken cocoons. If you spot an Io Moth caterpillar, do not touch it! The branched spines may look soft and harmless, but they are actually venomous. If touched, they immediately cause a painful burning or itching sensation. While alarming, the pain and irritation rarely lasts more than a few hours

LUNA MOTH

Size: Large; wingspan of 4.0-4.5 inches

Where You'll See It: Eastern US and southeastern Canada.

What It Looks Like: Light green wings with a long hind wing tail and a white, furry body.

Adults are nocturnal and commonly attracted to artificial lights; they do not feed and don't have working mouthparts. When the moth flies, its long hind wing tails make a sound that confuses bats, causing them to target the long tails, often leaving its body unharmed. Adults also have fern-like antennae.

Caterpillars are bright green with yellow side stripe; the plump, full-grown caterpillars may be nearly 3 inches long; they spin papery cocoons on the forest floor.

POLYPHEMUS MOTH
Size: Large; wingspan of 4.0–5.8 inches

Where You'll See It: Throughout the US and southern Canada

What It Looks Like: Tan to reddish-brown wings with a large eyespot on each hind wing; males have large fern-like antennae.

This is one of the largest moths in North America; the obvious hind wing eyespots help scare predators or deflect their attack away from the moth's stout body.

The plump caterpillar is green with a brown head and yellow dashes along the sides. They reach nearly 3 inches long when fully grown. Each caterpillar spins a pale oval cocoon that is about the size of a chicken's egg. They are attached to branches with silk and hang downward, often making them easy to spot.

PANDORA SPHINX MOTH
Size: Large; wingspan of 3.2–4.5 inches

Where You'll See It: Eastern US and southeastern Canada

What It Looks Like: Long olive-green front wings with darker green patches and streaks of pink; olive-green hind wings with darker patches and a pale base; a long abdomen.

One of the country's most beautiful moths, this moth is mostly active during twilight. It uses its long tongue to feed at flowers, much like a hummingbird.

The light-green or reddish-brown caterpillars are chubby, with noticeable eyespots along the sides; unlike many other sphinx moths, the fully grown caterpillars lack a long, curved horn on their rear end. The caterpillars pupate underground.

HUMMINGBIRD CLEARWING

Size: Large; wingspan of 1.5–2.2 inches

Where You'll See It: Eastern US and southeastern Canada

What It Looks Like: Long reddish wings with large transparent patches, a greenish-yellow thorax and a darker abdomen.

This fuzzy moth flies during the day and looks like a bumblebee; its fast-moving wings even makes a buzzing noise. Adults hover at flowers like a hummingbird and use their long tongue to sip nectar.

The caterpillars are often yellow-green with a darker green head but can vary in color somewhat; they also have pale side stripes and a prominent curved horn on their rear end.

GIANT LEOPARD MOTH

Size: Large; wingspan of 2.5–3.5 inches

Where You'll See It: Eastern US and southeastern Canada

What It Looks Like: Large; elongated white front wings with a mix of solid black and hollow black spots.

There is absolutely no mistaking this moth when you see it; these large moths are common at artificial lights.

If disturbed, they often drop to the ground and temporarily play dead. When they do, they curl up their abdomen to reveal a bold orange-and-iridescent-blue pattern, and secrete a foul tasting liquid to deter predators.

The large hairy caterpillars are deep black with bright red rings on their body. Fully grown larvae may reach 3 inches long!

GARDEN TIGER MOTH

Size: Large; wingspan of 1.75–2.70 inches

Where You'll See It: Across southern Canada and the northern half of the United States; also found in Eurasia

What It Looks Like: Brown front wings with an intricate white pattern; back wings are orange with black spots; abdomen orange with black bands.

Due to its large size and beautiful color pattern, the Garden Tiger Moth is a very popular moth; it gets its name because it is a common sight in gardens. The adult moths are attracted to artificial lights at night.

The moth's caterpillars have a reddish brown coloring on their lower half; the larvae are often seen wandering along the ground in fall where they seek protected sites to overwinter.

PALE BEAUTY

Size: Medium-size; wingspan of 1.10–2.0 inches

Where You'll See It: Northern two-thirds of the US and southern Canada

What It Looks Like: Pale-green wings with two darkly outlined pale stripes; back wings with irregular borders; the tail is stubby.

Appropriately named, this small pretty moth has delicate wings that are pale green to almost white, and it holds its wings open while at rest.

The elongated brown inchworm caterpillars feed on a wide array of trees and shrubs—from evergreens to deciduous trees; it resembles a small twig. Unlike other geometer moth caterpillars, the Pale Beauty caterpillar has short hairs along the sides of its body, which help make it harder to see on plants.

EASTERN TENT CATERPILLAR MOTH

Size: Small; wingspan of 1.0–1.6 inches

Where You'll See It: Throughout the eastern US and southeastern Canada

What It Looks Like: Brown wings; the front wings have two pale parallel lines; adults rest with their wings over their back looking a little like a tent.

These moths get their name from the "tents" that their caterpillars create in trees; the tent consists of a silken web that looks a lot like a big clump of cotton candy; the tents provide protection and help regulate temperature.

The hungry caterpillars often completely strip trees of leaves but aren't usually a serious pest. The caterpillars eventually spin cocoons, but the caterpillars are noticed more often than the adults.

INCHWORM

Size: Highly variable; 0.5–1.5 inches long

Where You'll See It: Throughout the US

What It Looks Like: Generally green to brown; a smooth, long body with legs at both ends but none in the middle.

Inchworms are caterpillars of geometer moths, a large, diverse family with more than 1400 species occurring in North America. These caterpillars have short legs at both ends of their long body but none in the middle. They move by grasping a leaf or twig, then looping their body to pull along their rear end, almost as if they were measuring the distance.

If an Inchworm detects a predator, it escapes by jumping off the plant it's feeding on and hangs onto a silken lifeline. This is why you can sometimes spot them hanging in the breeze.

PLUME MOTH

Size: Small; wingspan of 0.50–1.50 inches

Where You'll See It: Throughout the US and much of Canada

What It Looks Like: Small, long, slim body and dull-colored narrow wings that look like a T when at rest.

This is a family of primarily small, drab moths; over 160 species of Plume Moths are found in North America. The adult moths have narrow wings that are deeply divided into feather-like lobes, giving the group its name.

Active during the day, these moths hold their wings out at a 90-degree angle in a T shape and resemble a small, dead twig.

BEES, WASPS, AND ANTS (Order *Hymenoptera*)

WESTERN HONEYBEE

Size: Small; 0.4–0.75 inch long

Where You'll See It: Throughout the US and southern Canada

What It Looks Like: Fuzzy, golden-orange body with a black-striped abdomen, large eyes, and clear, transparent wings.

This is probably the most well-known and common bee in the US. Native to Europe, it was brought to the US by early settlers. Today, bees help pollinate a variety of foods, from pumpkins to almonds.

Honeybees are social insects and live in a large groups called hives, which may contain up to 100,000 individuals. Each hive has one queen that lays all of the eggs.

Safety Note: Honeybees can sting, and they aggressively defend their hive.

AMERICAN BUMBLEBEE

Size: Medium-size; 0.6–1 inch long

Where You'll See It: Throughout much of the eastern US west to the Rocky Mountains and southeastern Canada

What It Looks Like: Large; fuzzy black and yellow body with black transparent wings and large dark eyes; often have yellow "baskets" of pollen on their hind legs.

These round, somewhat chubby insects are easy to spot because they are fuzzy and have black-and-yellow banding.

Bumblebees live in relatively small, underground hives that last for one year. These bees are important pollinators of many wild plants and food crops.

Safety Note: Bumblebees are not aggressive, but they can sting, especially if defending their nest.

LEAFCUTTER BEE

Size: Small; 0.40 0.75 inch long

Where You'll See It: Throughout the US and southern Canada

What It Looks Like: Stout, compact blackish-brown bodies often with white or golden hairs, transparent wings, and pale bands on the abdomen.

While these native solitary bees are small, the signs of their activity in the landscape are easy to spot: adults cut semicircular pieces out of leaves. The adults carry the leaf pieces back to their nests, using them to line the "rooms" for their larvae. Adults have powerful jaws for cutting leaves.

Females place a mass of pollen mixed with nectar in each "room" of the nest then lay an egg on each mass; the worm-like larvae feed on the pollen as they grow.

STRIPED SWEAT BEE
Size: Small; 0.40–0.50 inch long

Where You'll See It: Throughout the US and southern Canada

What It Looks Like: The head and thorax are metallic green; dark wings; the abdomen is metallic green or yellow with black bands.

These relatively small bees are typically shiny metallic green with varying degrees of yellow and black banding. These bees are common visitors to flowers and important pollinators, and they nest in the ground, building underground tunnels and chambers in which their young complete development.

Females collect pollen, gather it together with nectar to form a large ball, place it in an individual cell, and lay an egg. The resulting pollen mass is all the food needed to support the developing larva.

BALD-FACED HORNET
Size: Small; 0.50–0.75 inch long

Where You'll See It: Throughout most of the US and southern Canada

What It Looks Like: Mostly black with some whitish markings and a distinctive white face; transparent (see-through) wings.

Despite its name, this is actually a wasp, not a hornet (hornets are larger). These wasps build papery egg-shaped nests in trees or tall shrubs; nests are often concealed amongst vegetation; they may be hard to see until late fall when branches are bare.

Adults are predators of many other insects and arthropods.

Safety Note: These wasps will aggressively defend their nests; their stings are painful; never closely approach or aggravate an active colony.

MUD DAUBER WASP

Size: Medium-size; 0.75–1.0 inch long

Where You'll See It: Throughout the US and southern Canada.

What It Looks Like: Usually has a black to metallic bluish-black body often with yellow markings; a long, narrow waist.

This entertaining group of wasps is famous for building nests made of mud, often forming elaborate tubes, masses or pot-like structures. Female wasps collect small balls of mud with their jaws and transport it to the nest site. Once the nest is finished, the female collects small prey, including other insects and spiders, placing a prey item in each cell of the nest, where they serve as food for the larvae.

While Mud Daubers are considered beneficial insects, their nests can be a nuisance when built on homes or other buildings.

PAPER WASP

Size: Large; 0.70–1.0 inch long

Where You'll See It: Throughout the US and southern Canada; nests are often constructed near homes, particularly near roof edges

What It Looks Like: Variable; slender brown, reddish-brown to black bodies marked with yellow, dark transparent wings; a narrow waist and pointed abdomen.

Paper Wasps are social insects that build brown papery nests, which are constructed by combining chewed wood and plant material with saliva (spit). Adult wasps are highly beneficial, as being both pollinators and predators.

Safety Note: Adults can inflict a painful sting if handled and aggressively defend their nest if provoked.

YELLOW JACKET

Size: Medium-size; 0.40–0.60 inch long

Where You'll See It: Throughout the US and southern Canada

What It Looks Like: Stout body with yellow-and-black markings and narrow, amber wings.

Yellow jackets are wasps that are regularly mistaken for bees. Their paper-like nests are made from chewed wood and saliva; they frequently nest in or around buildings or in the ground.

Adult yellow jackets are fond of sugary food and investigate open soda cans, juice bottles, or cut fruit. As a result, they may be a minor nuisance at picnics or other outdoor gatherings. Adults are predators and scavengers, feeding larvae a diet of live or dead arthropods; they also regularly visit flowers for nectar.

Safety Note: Yellow Jackets aggressively defend their nests and will attack if disturbed. They can inflict a painful sting, so be cautious if you spot one and don't approach an active nest.

CARPENTER ANT

Size: Small; 0.30–0.50 inch long

Where You'll See It: Throughout the US and southern Canada

What It Looks Like: Black to red-brown ant with a rounded thorax; large jaws.

Several species found in North America. While they vary in size they are all some of the largest ants you'll encounter.

Carpenter Ants nest in wood and use their jaws to dig elaborate tunnels. They can be found in dead and decaying logs and trees, but they occasionally nest in homes or buildings, where they can cause damage. Worker ants are most active outside the nest at night, when they are seen on the ground in search of small insects.

PAVEMENT ANT
Size: Small; 0.10–0.15 inch long

Where You'll See It: Northern two-thirds of the US and southern Canada

What It Looks Like: Body is dark brown to black.

Initially introduced from Europe over a century ago, these familiar ants have spread to over 25 states and are continuing to expand their range. These tiny ants usually nest under stones, logs, or boards but are also frequently seen along cracks in driveways or sidewalks where they made conical anthills.

Pavement Ants feed on many different foods, including dead insects, seeds, sugar, and fruit. They occasionally make their way into homes, often showing up in kitchens.

RED IMPORTED FIRE ANT
Size: Small; 0.15–0.25 inch long

Where You'll See It: Throughout the southern third of the US

What It Looks Like: Reddish-brown body with a black rear end.

The Red Imported Fire Ant is among the most abundant and disliked insects in the country; accidentally introduced from Brazil some 70 years ago, it has spread across much of the southern US. They are highly destructive pests, causing damage to building, crops, livestock and native wildlife.

A social species, it creates large subterranean colonies that are easy to spot because of their dome-shaped mound of soil.

Safety Note: The adults are highly aggressive; they will quickly pour out of disturbed nests, and they will sting repeatedly, producing a painful, burning sensation. Avoid stepping on nests or going near them.

BOXELDER BUG
Size: Small; 0.40–0.50 inch long

Where You'll See It: Throughout the US and southern Canada

What It Looks Like: Dull black flat oval body; reddish-orange stripes on the thorax and wing bases.

This colorful bug is closely associated with boxelder trees, its main host. Both adults and nymphs have piercing-sucking mouthparts and feed on the sap from leaves and developing seeds.

In fall, they seek out protected areas to overwinter; they may often congregate on the sunlit sides of homes and buildings in large numbers, making their way into walls where they hibernate. On warmer days, they can sometimes be found inside; they don't pose any danger to people, but they can release a smelly odor when disturbed or squished.

GREEN STINKBUG
Size: Medium-size; 0.50–0.70 inch long

Where You'll See It: Throughout the US and southern Canada

What It Looks Like: A bright-green body that is flattened and shield-shaped.

These bright-green insects use their beak-like mouthparts to pierce plants and suck out internal juices. When many green stink bugs are present, they can be a crop and garden pest.

Stinkbugs get their unflattering name because they can release a stinky-smelling chemical from specialized abdominal glands when threatened.

The colorful, oval-shaped nymphs are generally black with some red, green or yellow markings and lack wings; young nymphs tend to stay together and feed in groups.

SPINED SOLDIER BUG
Size: Medium-size; 0.45–0.60 inch long

Where You'll See It: Throughout the US and southern Canada

What It Looks Like: Spotted brown color; a shield-shaped body, one spine on each shoulder and a dark diamond on the hind end where the wings overlap.

Named for its prominent, pointed shoulders and predatory behavior, this insect is one of the most common and beneficial stinkbugs in North America. A hunter in all life stages, it feeds on many different soft-bodied insects, including many pests such as moth and beetle larvae. When hunting, it uses is sharp piercing-sucking mouthparts to harpoon its victims, inject digestive enzymes and slurp up the liquefied body contents

Adults spend the winter in protected locations, such as under leaf litter, bark, or mulch.

JAGGED AMBUSH BUG
Size: Medium-size; 0.40–0.50 inch long

Where You'll See It: Throughout the US and southern Canada

What It Looks Like: Color varies but often golden-yellow, brown or cream with darker patches or bands; violin-shaped body with enlarged grasping front legs.

The Jagged Ambush Bug's body has irregular, ragged edges. A highly camouflaged predator, it matches the color of the flower on which it is on, waiting motionless for visiting insects. When one arrives, the ambush bug catches it with its praying mantis–like arms, quickly immobilizing it by injecting venom, and then slurps out the liquefied body contents. Even though an ambush bug is small, its powerful venom enables it to capture insects much larger than itself, including honeybees, bumblebees, wasps, and butterflies. It is considered a highly beneficial predator.

WHEEL BUG

Size: Large; 1.0–1.25 inches long

Where You'll See It: Southern two-thirds of the US; more common in the East

What It Looks Like: Gray-brown body with long legs and antennae; a narrow head and prominent spiny rounded ridge on the back; wings folded flat over the abdomen.

This alien-looking insect is the largest assassin bug found in North America. Like other assassin bugs, it is a predator and uses its long front legs to grab unsuspecting prey and then injects a toxin with sharp, beaklike mouthparts that liquefies the prey's internal organs. It then slurps out the fluid. It can successfully capture butterflies, bumblebees, and other much larger insects. Wheel bugs are considered highly beneficial predators.

Safety Note: While not aggressive, wheel bugs can inflict a painful bite if handled.

LEAF-FOOTED BUG

Size: Large; 0.75–1.0 inch long

Where You'll See It: Throughout the US and southern Canada

What It Looks Like: Narrow brown body with long antennae; wings folded over the back; leaf-like projections on back legs.

These large insects are commonly spotted on plants. Because adults can fly, adults often also land on window sills, siding, or houses. They get their unique name from the distinctive flattened projections on their long hind legs that resemble leaves. They have long piercing-sucking mouthparts to puncture leaves, stems or fruit and drink plant juices. Adults spend the winter in larger groups in sheltered sites, including in buildings, woodpiles, or under mulch.

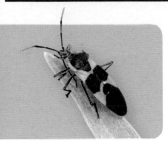

LARGE MILKWEED BUG
Size: Medium-size; 0.40–0.60 inch long

Where You'll See It: Throughout much of the US and southeastern Canada but generally absent in the Northwest

What It Looks Like: Elongated orange and black body with long black antennae.

The Large Milkweed Bug can be found feeding on milkweed plants. It uses it piercing-sucking mouthparts to sip juices from the plant, absorbing toxic chemicals from the plant into its body. The toxins help protect the bug, and its obvious orange-and-black coloration is a warning to predators that it tastes bad.

The adults and nymphs feed in groups on milkweed plants, northern populations are migratory, traveling south to overwinter in warmer southern locations.

Large Milkweed Bugs are easy to raise as pets; they love to eat sunflower seeds.

TARNISHED PLANT BUG
Size: Small; 0.18–0.25 inch long

Where You'll See It: Throughout the US and southern Canada

What It Looks Like: Oval, somewhat flat yellow-brown body with dark markings; long antennae.

These small insects are members of a large and diverse family of true bugs that mostly feed on plants.

The Tarnished Plant Bug gets its name for its dull appearance, which is similar to tarnished metal. These bugs can eat many different kinds of plants and transmit diseases, making them a serious pest.

As winter approaches, the adult bugs seek shelter in plant debris, or leaf litter, hibernating until the following spring.

GIANT WATER BUG

Size: Large; 1.75–2.50 inches long

Where You'll See It: Throughout the US and southern Canada; freshwater ponds, lakes, and flooded ditches

What It Looks Like: Large, flat oval body with large, pincer-like front legs; it looks like a large cockroach.

These bugs are sit-and-wait predators, hanging out in submerged vegetation at the edges of wetlands; they can breathe underwater using a snorkel-like siphon from their rear end.

Ferocious predators of insects, fish, frogs, and other aquatic organisms, adults grab prey with their powerful front legs, inject a digestive toxin using a short, pointed beak, and suck out the liquefied remains. Giant Water Bugs are the largest true bugs in the United States. They are often attracted to artificial lights.

Safety Note: Don't touch! These bugs can inflict a painful bite.

WATER BOATMAN

Size: Small; 0.20–0.45 inch long

Where You'll See It: Throughout the US and southern Canada

What It Looks Like: spotted brown; somewhat flattened oval body; large eyes; paddle-like hind legs.

These unusual aquatic insects are good swimmers. They have strong, highly specialized hind legs that look like oars, which help them propel themselves forward in a quick somewhat jerky motion.

Their front legs are short and adapted for collecting algae and other microorganisms. These insects can breathe underwater, much like a scuba diver; they do so by carrying a bubble of air around their abdomen.

WATER STRIDER
Size: Small; 0.3–0.5 inch long

Where You'll See It: Throughout the US and much of Canada

What It Looks Like: Brown narrow body with long middle and hind legs; found on the surface of water.

These amazing insects move effortlessly across the surface of water, much like miniature skaters. They do so because their long legs that help distribute their weight, and they are coated in fine hairs that repel water. Water striders are predators or scavengers that feed on living and dead insects, including many that accidentally fall into the water.

Because of their small size and delicate bodies, Water striders are easy to miss. Once spotted, they are very entertaining to watch but will scurry away quickly if approached too closely.

LEAFHOPPER
Size: Small; 0.15–0.75 inch long

Where You'll See It: Throughout the US and much of Canada

What It Looks Like: Narrow wedge-shaped bodies; color varies a lot; some are drab while others are brightly colored.

Leafhoppers are a diverse group of small, plant-dwelling insects. Both adults and nymphs feed on plant sap, using their piercing-sucking mouthparts to penetrate the living tissues of leaves and stems. Leafhoppers are common, but their small size and camouflaged appearance make them easy to overlook.

They have excellent vision and can readily hop to another leaf with their strong back legs. Leafhoppers communicate with each other using vibrations generated from their abdomen. These signals are too faint for humans to hear, but travel along the surface of plants to other leafhoppers.

PLANTHOPPER

Size: Small; 0.10—0.25 inch long

Where You'll See It: Throughout the US and much of Canada

What It Looks Like: Highly variable in color and form; white, brown or green; wide wings held vertically; some distinctly wedge-shaped.

Like Aphids (see next page), Planthoppers are small insects that feed on plant juices and excrete honeydew as a waste product. Planthoppers are a diverse group, with over 900 species found in the United States.

Adults tend to vary considerably in color and appearance, often with green, leaf-like membranous wings and other thorn-like projections; some even produce waxy secretions to help conceal their appearance. They tend to rely on camouflage for protection, often remaining still or moving slow to avoid detection but can readily hop if needed, as their name suggests.

SPITTLEBUG

Size: Small; 0.25—0.40 inch long

Where You'll See It: Throughout the US and much of Canada

What It Looks Like: White frothy mass on plants; the insect feeds inside, hidden from sight.

Spittlebugs might be the most common insects that most people haven't actually seen. Nonetheless, most of us however are familiar with the white frothy "spit" sometimes seen on plants. Inside this bubbly mass is an immature Spittlebug.

The developing pale nymphs feed on plant juices and pump air into their fluid secretions, creating the spit-like mass that protects them and prevents them from drying out. The resulting adults, called froghoppers, are good jumpers and can also fly.

APHID

Size: Very small; 0.10–0.15 inch long

Where You'll See It: Throughout the US and much of Canada

What It Looks Like: Oval body with a pair of pipe-like projections on the abdomen; color varies from green and yellow to orange, even black.

Easy to overlook because they are so tiny, aphids often look like small spots or eggs on plants. These common pear-shaped insects occur in colonies and use their piercing-sucking mouthparts to feed on plant juices; when there are many of them, they can damage leaves, stunt growth, or even kill plants.

Aphids are considered destructive pests of many ornamental plants and food crops. In the process of feeding, Aphids secrete a sugary liquid called honeydew; wasps, butterflies and ants feed on honeydew. In return for this sugar-rich treat, ants often protect and care for their aphid companions.

WOOLLY APHID

Size: Small; 0.08–0.15 inch long

Where You'll See It: Throughout the US and much of Canada

What It Looks Like: Pear-shaped body covered with white waxy filaments.

These bizarre insects always look like they're having a bad hair day. Woolly Aphids are famous for producing the waxy secretions that cover their bodies and give them an overall fuzzy, cotton-like appearance. These filaments help protect them from predators. Like other aphids, they feed in colonies on plant sap and generate honeydew, a sugary waste product.

Woolly Aphids are preyed upon by harvester butterfly caterpillars, the only carnivorous butterfly species in North America.

CICADA

Size: Large; 1.0–2.0 inches long

Where You'll See It: Throughout the US and southern Canada

What It Looks Like: Thick body with big, widely spaced eyes and clear wings.

These big bugs have large eyes and sort of look like giant flies; there are many different species, but all Cicada adults spend much of their time hidden in trees or plants, where males produce loud, high-pitched calls to attract females.

The immature nymphs live underground, feeding for several years on plant roots and developing; some, called periodical cicadas in eastern North America, take 13–17 years to complete development, emerging all at specific times. They emerge, and molt, leaving behind a paper-brown shell behind.

BEETLES (Order *Coleoptera*)

CLICK BEETLE

Size: Large; 0.5–1.2 inches long

Where You'll See It: Throughout the US and much of Canada

What It Looks Like: Varies in color and size with many species being brown to black; long, often dull or unmarked body.

While often drab, Click Beetles are fun to watch; they readily play dead when threatened. They get their name because they can arch back and "click" forward, propelling the insect several inches into the air. This sudden leap, along with the loud click, startles predators, and even humans.

Some species, like the Eyed Elater, are nearly two inches long and have large, false eyespots on their back.

GREEN JUNE BEETLE

Size: Medium-size; 0.6–1.0 inch long

Where You'll See It: Throughout much of the eastern US and southeastern Canada

What It Looks Like: Thick, oval body; adults are a dull, metallic green with a rust-colored stripe along the side.

This showy insect is considered a pest of grass, ornamental plants and various fruit crops, especially in large numbers. The worm-like grubs live underground during the day. They come to the surface at night to feed, leaving a small mound of dirt behind, and possibly damaging plants. Adults feed primarily on various fruits, including apples, peaches and berries.

Adults emerge in late spring, often in late May or June in many locations—which is why they are called June beetles. Adults have a slow, awkward flight and often fly until they bump into something.

GROUND BEETLE

Size: 0.25–1.25 inches long

Where You'll See It: Throughout the US and much of Canada

What It Looks Like: Most are shiny, brown to black and occasionally metallic; long, flat body; ridged wing covers; large jaws; long legs.

Ground Beetles are nocturnal predators that use their jaws to capture various insects and earthworms, slugs and snails; adults rarely fly but can run fast. While generally drab in color, some species are shiny and metallic-looking.

Ground Beetles can defend themselves by emitting unpleasant chemicals from the tip of their abdomen. A well-known example is the bombardier beetle, which can spray a jet of superheated fluid with great accuracy. Ground Beetle larvae live in the soil and are also predators.

FIREFLY

Size: Medium-size; 0.5–0.8 inch long

Where You'll See It: Eastern US and southern Canada

What It Looks Like: A flat black body with orange and yellow markings; underside tip of abdomen is pale and produces light.

Despite being called Fireflies or Lightning Bugs, Fireflies are actually beetles. Fireflies use a highly specialized organ in their body to light up and signal to potential mates. Each species of Firefly produces its own flashing pattern and some even flash simultaneously, creating a one-of-a-kind display.

Like Monarch Butterflies, Fireflies are toxic and want other animals to know it; the same is true for Firefly larvae (also known as glowworms). Fireflies use light to communicate, so they prefer dark places. Look for them in dark, open areas away from artificial lights at night.

JAPANESE BEETLE

Size: Small; 0.3–0.5 inch long

Where You'll See It: Mostly the eastern US and southeastern Canada

What It Looks Like: Metallic green with copper-colored wing coverings and white tufts along the abdomen; often feeds in groups.

As its name suggests, this shiny, oval-shaped beetle is native to Japan. It was accidentally introduced into the US in 1916 and has since spread to some 30 states. Like other invasive species, the adults have become a serious pest and causes millions of dollars in damage each year.

The white, grub-like larvae are a problem too, eating the roots of lawn grasses. Japanese Beetles can feed on more than 300 different plants.

LADY BEETLE

Size: Small; 0.25–0.4 inch long

Where You'll See It: Throughout the US and much of Canada

What It Looks Like: Oval; variable in color but often orange to red with black spots.

Also called Ladybugs or Ladybird Beetles, these small, shiny beetles are some of the most familiar and commonly encountered insects.

They are a diverse group, with over 400 species found in the United States. While their appearance varies by species, most have some combination of the recognizable orange, red or black-spotted color pattern. Generally, lady beetles are highly beneficial as both adults and larvae, being predators of many other small insects and insect eggs.

Adults of the introduced multicolored Asian Lady Beetle often invade homes and can deliver a somewhat painful bite. They have disrupted many native species, leading to population declines.

RED MILKWEED BEETLE

Size: Medium-size; 0.35–0.60 inch long

Where You'll See It: Northern half of the eastern US and southeastern Canada

What It Looks Like: Red body with black spots, black legs, and long black antennae.

These insects are always found by milkweed plants. Adult beetles feed on milkweed leaves and flower buds.

Like the Monarch Butterfly, the Red Milkweed Beetle incorporates toxic chemicals into its body, making them taste bad. Its bold red-and-black pattern lets predators know about this chemical defense. The beetle larvae live underground and feed on the roots of milkweed plants. When handled, adult beetles often make a squeaking noise.

METALLIC WOOD-BORING BEETLE
Size: Medium-size; 0.5–1.5 inches long

Where You'll See It: Throughout the US and much of Canada

What It Looks Like: Streamlined, bullet-shaped body; a flat head; short antennae; often has shiny metallic colors.

Metallic Wood-boring Beetles get their name from the bright, shiny colors often seen in adults. Active by day, they are often encountered at flowers, on vegetation, resting on logs, or even sitting on paths.

Female beetles seek out trees on which to lay eggs. Some wood-boring beetles can be extremely destructive pests. The emerald ash borer, which was accidentally introduced into the United States from Asia in the 1990s, is the most infamous example.

SOLDIER BEETLE
Size: Medium-size; 0.45–0.60 inch long

Where You'll See It: Throughout the US and southern Canada

What It Looks Like: Color and pattern varies; elongated, narrow body; the somewhat soft wing coverings don't completely cover the tip of the abdomen.

Soldier Beetles look like Fireflies, but they don't have the ability to produce light; due to their somewhat soft wing coverings, they are often called leatherwings. Active by day, Soldier Beetles are found at flowers and are common in summer and fall; in the eastern US, the yellow-and-black Goldenrod Soldier Beetle is particularly abundant on various flowers, particularly goldenrod. Many species are predatory and feed on small insects, while others prefer pollen and nectar. Most soldier beetles are beneficial.

Adult beetles defend themselves by secreting gross-tasting chemicals from glands on their body. Their bright coloration helps alert potential predators that they don't taste good.

TIGER BEETLE

Size: Medium-size; 0.50–0.90 inch long

Where You'll See It: Throughout the US and much of Canada; on the ground

What It Looks Like: Shiny, often iridescent, patterned body; large eyes; long legs; big jaws.

Tiger Beetles get their name because they are ferocious hunters. Typically found in a variety of open, sandy habitats, they are built for speed, and they hunt their prey by running them down. Tiger Beetles often have bright shiny colors, but approaching them can be hard as they have good vision and they often fly off.

Tiger Beetles are the fastest terrestrial insects in the world, moving so quickly that their vision blurs. As a result, they have to pause periodically when running to visually locate their prey. Tiger Beetle larvae live in the ground and are also predators.

REDDISH-BROWN STAG BEETLE

Size: Large; 2.0–2.8 inches long

Where You'll See It: Eastern US and extreme southeastern Canada

What It Looks Like: Shiny, dark brown to reddish-brown body; males with large, pincer-like mandibles.

Truly unmistakable in size and appearance, the Giant Stag Beetle is named for its mandibles (jaws), which resemble antlers. Males use their jaws to joust with rivals for access to mates and to fight predators. Females are similar in size but have much smaller jaws.

Adults don't use their jaws to catch food; instead, they eat tree sap and the juice from fermenting fruit. The large grayish-white larvae live in rotting logs and stumps.

Safety Note: Be careful; adult beetles can give a strong pinch.

GREATER BEE FLY

Size: Small; 0.5–0.7 inch long

Where You'll See It: Throughout the US and southern Canada

What It Looks Like: Compact, dark body covered with dense golden hairs; transparent (see-through) wings with a dark leading edge that are held outward, and a long, forward-pointing proboscis (a tongue-like structure).

These distinctive, cuddly-looking flies look like miniature bumble-bees; they hover like a hummingbird in front of each flower and use their long, stiff tongue to sip out the sugary nectar. Adults hover low to the ground as they feed, moving from one flower to another; they perch with their wings outstretched; often make a faint buzzing sound when flying.

Females lay eggs in the underground nests of solitary bees; the larvae then eat the unfortunate immature bees inside the nest.

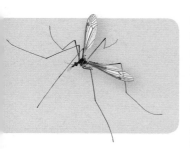

CRANE FLY

Size: Medium-size; 0.5–2.5 inches long

Where You'll See It: Throughout the US and much of Canada

What It Looks Like: Slender body with extremely long, thin legs; two wings.

At first glance, Crane Flies may look like huge mosquitoes, but they don't bite and are harmless. In fact, most adults eat very little, if anything!

These insects are named for their extremely long, delicate legs, which suspend their equally narrow body high above them, much like a crane. Adult Crane Flies have a slow, somewhat bouncing, flight, especially when in your house or against an outside wall.

Crane Fly larvae live in moist habitats or are aquatic; some feed on decaying plants, others are predators of aquatic organisms, including mosquito larvae, and some are even lawn pests.

DEERFLY

Size: Small; 0.25–0.40 inch long

Where You'll See It: Throughout the US and much of Canada

What It Looks Like: Color varies; brown to yellow or black body; large often brightly colored eyes; banded wings.

These small, often yellow-and-black-striped flies are frequently considered a nuisance because they attack mammals, including cattle, deer, dogs and humans. They can even bite the same victim over and over again. Deerflies are attracted by body heat, carbon dioxide, and visual signals, such as motion.

Like mosquitoes, female Deerflies require blood to produce viable (hatchable) eggs. Females use their blade-like mouthparts to cut the skin before lapping up the blood produced; the result is a painful and annoying bite. There are over 100 different species of Deerflies in the continental United States.

FLESH FLY

Size: Small; 0.35–0.5 inch long

Where You'll See It: Throughout the US and much of Canada

What It Looks Like: Gray body with longitudinal black stripes, a bristly abdomen, and reddish eyes.

These common flies are found throughout North America. They are similar in appearance to house flies but typically a bit larger. Flesh flies get their kind of gross name because their larvae (known as maggots) typically feed on decaying material, dung, dead organisms, even wounds on animals.

The drab bristly adults feed on nectar, sap, and other sugary substances using their sponge-like mouthparts to lap up the liquid meal. They may be frequently encountered at flowers.

HOUSE FLY

Size: Small; 0.15–0.35 inches

Where You'll See It: Throughout the US and much Canada

What It Looks Like: Gray hairy body with four black stripes on the thorax; transparent wings and red eyes.

A familiar bug, house flies live among humans and are often considered a pest, frequently landing on food; commonly found in and around homes.

House Flies are strongly attracted by garbage, animal waste and decaying organic matter on which they may feed and lay eggs. Adult house flies don't bite. Instead they have sponge-like mouthparts to sop up liquids and are especially fond of sugary foods.

ROBBER FLY

Size: Medium-size; 0.3–1.0 inches

Where You'll See It: Throughout the US and much of Canada

What It Looks Like: Highly variable in size and color; often slender body with a pointed abdomen, large eyes, and long, bristly legs.

Like miniature hawks, Robber Flies are ferocious predators and use their large eyes and good vision to hunt prey. They perch on plants and then fly out to snag passing insects with their long, barbed legs. Once prey is caught, they inject it with saliva; the saliva paralyzes the insect and breaks down the body contents into a liquid that can be easily consumed.

Robber Flies are members of a large and diverse family with more than 7000 species found worldwide. Some species mimic bees and wasps in their appearance.

LOVEBUG

Size: Small; 0.25–0.35 inches

Where You'll See It: Throughout the southeastern US

What It Looks Like: Small, dull black wings; an orange thorax and long legs.

Lovebugs are a common sight during the summer months across the southeastern US; actually small flies, these insects are closely related to mosquitoes and may be just an annoying to many people.

The adult flies are typically seen while mating, hence the name "lovebug," and the male and female lock onto one another and remain together for several days, even while flying. Sometimes appearing in huge numbers, they can make their way into houses or splatter against the windshields of cars. Fortunately, the adults do not bite or sting and live for only a few days.

MOSQUITO

Size: Small; 0.20–0.35 inches

Where You'll See It: Throughout the US and Canada

What It Looks Like: Narrow, often striped body with two wings; long thin legs and a prominent, needle-like proboscis to pierce the skin.

Well known for their high-pitched buzz and itchy bites, Mosquitoes are among the most irritating backyard insects; they can be very numerous. Actually small flies, mosquitoes are a diverse insects group; adults are active fliers and feed on flower nectar and other sugary foods.

Female Mosquitoes need blood to make eggs. They find hosts by using a combination of vision, smell and temperature. Mosquitoes breed in or near standing water and only need a spoonful to reproduce. Be sure to regularly get rid of standing water in any potential breeding sites, such as flower pots or other containers.

MOSQUITO LARVA
Size: Small; 0.10–0.20 inch long

Where You'll See It: Throughout the US and Canada.

What It Looks Like: Long brown segmented body; many hairs, but no legs; an enlarged thorax and a long breathing siphon from its behind.

Mosquito Larvae live in water; they are commonly found in many wetlands but prefer shallow water and can breed in everything from fountains and birdbaths to flower pots and old tires. The long, skinny larvae spend most of their lives close to the water surface. They breathe through a long tube called a siphon and dangle with their heads down, using their fan-like mouthparts to eat algae, bacteria, and other microorganisms. Mosquito Larvae are often called wigglers due to their frequent back-and-forth thrashing movement in the water.

DRAGONFLIES AND DAMSELFLIES (Order *Odonata*)

COMMON WHITETAIL
Size: Large; 1.6–1.9 inches

Where You'll See It: Throughout the US and southern Canada

What It Looks Like: Thick; male with a brown thorax, brown eyes, four transparent wings with a wide black central band, and a long, white abdomen; female with three black spot bands on the wings and a brown abdomen with white dashes.

This is one of the most recognizable dragonflies. Dragonflies use their good vision and fast flight to catch insects; they use their spiny, outstretched legs to catch prey in mid-air. Dragonfly nymphs (naiads) are aquatic and also predators.

EASTERN AMBERWING

Size: Large; 0.8–1.0 inch

Where You'll See It: Throughout the eastern US and southeastern Canada

What It Looks Like: Brown body with four transparent orange-to-amber wings, elongated, pale striped brown abdomen and large eyes.

This common species is the second-smallest dragonfly in the United States. As its name suggests, the Eastern Amberwing has short, somewhat stubby wings that are orange-to-amber in color, especially in males; females have transparent wings banded with brown. This dragonfly's noticeably banded abdomen mimics the appearance of a wasp.

This wasp disguise is enhanced by its behavior: When perched, it flicks its wings and abdomen up and down in an attempt to fool would-be predators that it a stinging insect to be avoided.

EASTERN PONDHAWK

Size: Large; 1.50–2.0 inches

Where You'll See It: Throughout the eastern US and southeastern Canada

What It Looks Like: Male has powdery blue body, long, narrow abdomen, large eyes and four transparent wings held out to the side; female has a bright green body and an abdomen banded with black.

This large, colorful species is common throughout much of the eastern two-thirds of the United States. They are called pond-hawks because the adults are aggressive hunters. Like other dragonflies, they have excellent vision and quickly dart out from their perch to capture passing insects.

The naiads (dragonfly larvae) complete development underwater. When fully grown, they crawl out of the water onto vegetation, a dead branch or rock and molt into a winged adult.

HALLOWEEN PENNANT

Size: Large; 1.0–1.7 inches

Where You'll See It: Eastern two-thirds of the US and southeastern Canada

What It Looks Like: Long brown abdomen with an orange top stripe; large eye; four transparent amber-colored wings have wide dark-brown-to-black bands and spots.

This beautiful dragonfly is named for its noticeably orange and black wings that seem perfect for Halloween. Like other dragonflies, it is an active aerial hunter, preying on many flying insects, including mosquitoes. Adults perch on dead branches or other vegetation and fly out to catch passing insects. These dragonflies are highly beneficial insects that help to keep many annoying insects under control.

EBONY JEWELWING

Size: Large; wingspan of 1.5–2.25 inches

Where You'll See It: Throughout the eastern two-thirds of the US and southeastern Canada

What It Looks Like: Males have narrow, rounded solid black wings. Females have more bronze-colored wings with a white spot on each wingtip; both have an iridescent greenish-blue body; large for a damselfly.

Adults have a relatively slow, fluttering flight. They are often found resting on low-growing leaves or branches in sunny forest spots near streams or small rivers and typically only fly a short distance when disturbed.

These damselflies have large eyes and can turn their head to watch for predators or prey; they stretch out their long legs out like a basket to catch flying prey. Adults don't live very long, surviving for only about 2 weeks.

CAROLINA GRASSHOPPER
Size: Large; 1.20–2.0 inches long

Where You'll See It: Throughout most of the US and southern Canada

What It Looks Like: Mottled grayish to brown; body is elongated.

These large grasshoppers are well camouflaged, enabling them to blend.

Adults readily fly up, revealing their conspicuous cream-bordered black back wings, and they may make a noticeable flapping noise. At first glance, flying Carolina Grasshoppers may resemble a large butterfly. But the adults quickly land again on the ground several yards ahead. The species feeds on a number of different plants and grasses and can be a minor pest in years when they are abundant. Female Carolina Grasshoppers lay their eggs in clusters called pods in the soil.

KATYDID
Size: Large; 0.50–2.70 inches long

Where You'll See It: Throughout the US and southern Canada

What It Looks Like: Green body with large hind legs and long thin antennae; may have large wings; females have an obvious ovipositor (for laying eggs).

There are more than 250 Katydid species in the US, and many look like large green crickets at first glance. They are primarily nocturnal and spend their time hidden in plants; both adults and nymphs feed on plants. They are probably best known though for their distinctive raspy courtship calls, which are produced primarily by males who rub both front wings together, a process called stridulation. While calls vary tremendously between species this insect's name comes from the call of the common True Katydid. As males start to call, neighboring individuals often chime in too, so it sounds like "katy-did, katy-didn't."

FALL FIELD CRICKET
Size: Large; 0.75–1.25 inches long

Where You'll See It: Throughout the US and southern Canada

What It Looks Like: Oval black body with brown wings, large hind legs, long antennae, and two prominent tail filaments; females have a long sword-like extension on the called an ovipositor (for laying eggs).

These musical insects are heard more often than seen. To attract mates, male crickets sing by rubbing their wings together. The resulting chirps are a familiar part of summer nights.

Crickets often hide under objects or amid plants during the day; adults and nymphs are good jumpers and can get away quickly if disturbed. Adults wander their way into homes and buildings. Adults and nymphs are omnivores, feeding on fresh and decaying plant material and insects.

NORTHERN MOLE CRICKET
Size: Large; 1.0–1.70 inches long

Where You'll See It: The central and eastern US into southeastern Canada

What It Looks Like: Brown, long body with shovel-like front legs; hind wings extend beyond the tip of the abdomen.

Mole Crickets have streamlined bodies with shovel-like front legs perfect for digging, and a well-armored thorax for shaping and packing soil. They dig tunnels and spend much of their lives underground. Like other crickets, the males produce chirping calls to attract females and construct special burrows with widened openings to help amplify the sound, much like a trumpet.

Three species of Mole Crickets were accidentally introduced into the US; they are pests of grasses and other crops and found in warmer parts of the country, from Florida to California.

AMERICAN COCKROACH

Size: Large; 1.0–1.5 inches long

Where You'll See It: Much of the US and into southern Canada

What It Looks Like: Large; oval reddish-brown body with spiny legs and long, slender antennae; adults have brown wings and a pale-edged shield behind the head.

This common insect has adapted well to living with humans and is considered an undesirable pest. While usually found outdoors, they can invade homes and buildings when looking for food.

When inside, they tend to prefer warm, dark, and moist locations; they are primarily active at night and seldom venture out into open areas during the day.

EARWIG

Size: Medium-size, 0.5–0.75 inch long

Where You'll See It: Throughout the US and much of Canada

What It Looks Like: Long dark to reddish-brown body; long antennae; prominent pinchers on the end of the abdomen.

Despite their name, these weird-looking insects do not burrow into the ears of unsuspecting people. Instead, they are scavengers for food or prey upon other small organisms. Earwigs have distinctive pincher-like features (known as cerci) on their rear end; they are more obvious and curved in males. The cerci are used for defense, as well as to help capture prey.

Female earwigs are good mothers. They protect their nest and provide food for their developing young. Adult earwigs occasionally venture into homes, basements or garages.

CADDISFLY

Size: Small; 0.25–1.25 inches long

Where You'll See It: Throughout the US and much of Canada

What It Looks Like: Narrow body with drab wings; very long, thin antennae. Caddisflies look like dull-colored moths.

Although closely related to butterflies and moths, Caddisflies have wings that are covered with fine, dense hairs instead of the scales found in butterflies and moths. The adults are active fliers and commonly attracted to light at night. When at rest, they hold their wings over their back in a characteristic roof-like posture.

Caddisfly larvae are aquatic; they inhabit the bottoms of rivers and streams to ponds and lakes. Once larvae develop, they tube-shaped cases by weaving twigs, sand, small stones, and other debris together with silk.

DOBSONFLIES AND FISHFLIES (Order *Megaloptera*)

EASTERN DOBSONFLY

Size: Large; 4.0–5.5 inches long

Where You'll See It: Throughout the eastern US and southeastern Canada

What It Looks Like: Large; elongated brown body with large gray-brown wings; males have long, tusk-like curved jaws.

Like something out of a scary movie, the Eastern Dobsonfly is ferocious-looking. Adults approach 6 inches in length, and their long, curved pincher-like jaws of the males look spooky! Despite their big jaws, the males are completely harmless; the females have short but strong jaws that are can deliver a painful bite.

If disturbed, adults rear their head back and flex their jaws, warning any attacker to think twice.

ANTLION

Size: Large; 0.8–1.5 inches long

Where You'll See It: Throughout the US and southern Canada

What It Looks Like: Long, skinny body with short antennae; large, heavily veined wings, often with darker markings.

Adult Antlions are weak fliers and feed primarily on flower nectar and pollen. Antlion larvae are ferocious predators; they dig deep pits to trap unsuspecting ants or other small insects. Resembling a cone-shaped hole, the pits are constructed in sandy soil and easy to spot. Most passing ants that fall in the pit slide down the sides and into the larva's jaws; if prey tries to escape, the antlion throws sand at it to knock it back down.

Antlion larvae have powerful jaws to capture their prey; they inject venom and suck out the liquefied contents.

GREEN LACEWING

Size: Small; 0.4–0.7 inch long

Where You'll See It: Throughout the US and much of Canada

What It Looks Like: Slender, light green body with long antennae, prominent golden eyes and clear transparent lacy-looking wings with green venation.

These delicate insects help gardeners, as their alligator-looking larvae eat many plant pests. As a result, they are sold commercially for release in home landscapes, greenhouses or gardens.

Adult Green Lacewings are weak fliers; they feed primarily on flower nectar and pollen as well as sugary secretions from aphids called honeydew.

MAYFLY

Size: Small; 0.25-1.0 inches long, not including tail filaments

Where You'll See It: Throughout the U.S. and much of Canada

What It Looks Like: Narrow pale to dark body; long legs; four wings held upright over the back; two to three long filaments off the abdomen.

Mayflies are fragile-looking insects that exhibit two very different lifestyles. The immatures (nymphs) are completely aquatic, living at the bottom of fast-flowing streams or other freshwater habitats. When fully grown, they emerge from the water and molt twice before they can fly.

The swarms of adults can be so large that can shut down roads or even be seen on radar. Mayflies hold the record for the shortest adult life of any insect; most live less than a day.

PRAYING MANTIS
Size: Large, 2.0–4.0 inches long

Where You'll See It: Throughout much of the US and into southeastern Canada

What It Looks Like: Long thin green-to-brown body; triangular head; enlarged front legs for grasping prey.

The Praying Mantis is a remarkable insect. They sit motionlessly on plants waiting to ambush prey that gets too close. In the blink of an eye, the mantis reaches out with its powerful front legs, which are armed with spikes, and dinner is served.

Mantises live a relatively long time, and they can make good summer pets.

WALKING STICK
Size: Large; 3.0-3.6 inches

Where You'll See It: Throughout the U.S. and southern Canada

What It Looks Like: Long slender brown or green body; long legs and antennae; resembles a small twig or branch.

As their name suggests, walking sticks display amazing camouflage; both adults and immature walking sticks have extremely long legs and slender bodies resembling twigs or small branches.

Adults and nymphs are slow moving and feed on the leaves of various trees and shrubs. If threatened, some species have another trick: they can shoot out a foul-smelling chemical spray, and they can aim very well. Walking sticks are easy to care for and can make good summer pets.

SPIDERS (Order *Araneae*)

BLACK AND YELLOW GARDEN SPIDER
Size: Large; 0.75-2.5 inches

Where You'll See It: throughout the U.S. and extreme southern Canada

What It Looks Like: Egg-shaped abdomen with black-and-yellow markings; eight black legs marked with yellow or red; females are larger than males

This is one of the largest, most conspicuous and abundant orb-weaving spiders in the U.S. Adults build impressive circular webs, which may measure over two feet! Adults rest head-down in the web and wait for insects to get stuck. The vibration caused by the struggling insect alerts the spider, which wraps up the prey.

Safety Note: These spiders are mostly harmless, though can give a painful bite and should not be handled.

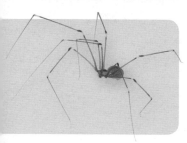

CELLAR SPIDER

Size: Medium-size; body is 0.25-0.35 inches; legs are much longer

Where You'll See It: Throughout the U.S. and southern Canada

What It Looks Like: Small oblong gray to brown body with eight very long thin legs.

Due to their long thin legs, these flimsy-looking spiders are often mistaken for daddy longlegs (which aren't actually spiders at all). Cellar spiders are true spiders and have a two-part body that consists of a cephalothorax and a distinct abdomen, eight eyes, and fang-like mouthparts.

These harmless spiders do not bite are commonly found in homes and spin silk, creating what appears to be disheveled, highly unorganized small webs for capturing prey. They build their webs in shady corners, basements, attics or under overhangs.

GREEN LYNX SPIDER

Size: Medium-size; 0.5-0.85 inches long

Where You'll See It: Throughout the southern half of the U.S.

What It Looks Like: Bright green body with eight somewhat paler legs with black spines and spots; females are much larger than males.

This beautiful, emerald-green predator is one of the most commonly encountered spiders in the southern U.S. Unlike many other spiders, it does not construct a web. Instead, the green lynx spider relies on camouflage and its good vision and speed to catch prey. Frequently spotted on flowers or poised at the top of weedy, shrubby vegetation, it patiently waits for insects.

In the fall, females construct one or more egg sacs, each often containing hundreds of eggs; she actively guards the eggs until they hatch and even helps the young spiders emerge.

JUMPING SPIDER

Size: Small; 0.15-0.60 inches

Where You'll See It: Throughout the U.S. and most of Canada

What It Looks Like: Thick, hairy body; eight eyes, but two of them are very large and face forward; the front four legs are longer than the others.

Despite their small size and somewhat adorable appearance, they are ferocious hunters. They actively search for food during the day, feeding on a wide range of other insects.

Spiders pounce on prey from a distance, often leaping many times their body length. Jumping spiders rely on blood pressure, not big muscles, to leap. They increase the bloodflow to their legs (insect blood is known as hemolymph), causing the legs to extend rapidly and propelling the spider forward.

CENTIPEDES (Class *Chilopoda*)

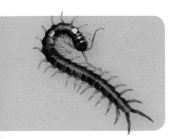

CENTIPEDES

Size: Large; 1.0-5.0 inches

Where You'll See It: Throughout the U.S. and much of Canada

What It Looks Like: Typically tan to dark brown; segmented worm-like bodies with many long legs.

Centipedes are long flat animals that look a little like aliens! Although their name literally means 100 legs, most have a lot less than that. They have only one pair of legs per segment, and the legs extend outward from their body. Nocturnal predators, they use their speed and venomous claws to feed on small insects, worms, and other critters.

Safety Note: Bites are uncommon, but painful; don't touch!

EARTHWORM

Size: Large; 4.0-8.0 inches

Where You'll See It: Throughout the U.S. and much of Canada

What It Looks Like: Long, cylindrical reddish-brown to pinkish body.

Unlike insects, earthworms do not have an exoskeleton. They instead have a fluid-filled body cavity surrounded by muscle. Earthworms breathe through their skin and require moist environments; they are highly beneficial decomposers and often improve the soil.

Earthworms are often spotted in good numbers moving across sidewalks or other surfaces on rainy days; instead of being "flooded out" the moist conditions help the worms travel, and move farther than they could in soil.

MILLIPEDE

Size: Medium-size; 0.50-6.0 inches

Where You'll See It: Throughout the U.S. and southern Canada

What It Looks Like: Dark, smooth cylindrical worm-like body with many small legs.

Millipedes are shiny, dark colored, worm-like creatures. Bearing two pairs of legs on each segment, they may have several hundred legs but crawl slowly on the ground. Millipedes are harmless and quite beneficial creatures, feeding on organic material and helping to recycle it.

When disturbed, millipedes stop moving and tightly coil up in defense.

HARVESTMEN

Size: Small; 0.15-0.30 inches; very long legs

Where You'll See It: Throughout the U.S. and much of Canada

What It Looks Like: Small round brown body; eight extremely long thin legs.

Also commonly called daddy longlegs, these animals aren't actually true spiders and are more closely related to scorpions. Unlike spiders, harvestmen only have two eyes and don't have fangs or make silk.

Harvestmen are nocturnal scavengers or predators and feed on everything from insects and slugs to fungi. Harvestmen get their name because they sometimes cluster together in large groups (often in the fall around harvest time). The legs of harvestmen break off easily and this helps them escape predators.

SOWBUGS AND PILLBUGS
Size: Small; 0.25-0.5 inches

Where You'll See It: Throughout the U.S. and southern Canada

What It Looks Like: Dark gray to brown; oval body with seven plate-like segments and seven pairs of legs.

Sowbugs and pillbugs are odd, primitive-looking creatures. Not insects at all, they are small, gray land-dwelling crustaceans related to crayfish. Resembling tiny armadillos, they have hard, shell-like coverings made up of plates and seven pairs of legs. While sowbugs and pillbugs are very similar, pillbugs can roll up into a ball when disturbed earning them the name "roly-pollies."

They are found under logs, rocks, and other dark, damp spots.

Projects and Activities

Moths and other insects drawn to a light

Attracting Insects with a Light

Many insects are active at night and can easily be attracted to artificial lights. Entomologists generally use blacklights, or ultraviolet (UV) lights, as these are more effective than traditional incandescent lights at drawing in a wider array of insects. Blacklights are relatively inexpensive and can be purchased from many entomological or scientific supply companies; they can be run of a portable battery or via an electrical outlet using an extension cord. A 20-watt self-ballasted fluorescent blacklight bulb is ideal as it screws into a normal light fixture. However, a basic incandescent light is easy to use if you do not have a blacklight available.

WHAT YOU'LL NEED

- An old white sheet

- A good length of rope or twine

- Two binder clips or clothespins

- A clamp light without the aluminum reflector. If you don't have this, a standard camping lantern will work.

- A 20-watt self-ballasted fluorescent blacklight bulb (can also use a 75-watt incandescent bulb)

- A long extension cord (100-foot length or longer)

- Two small rocks or bricks

- A large mouth plastic jar with a lid

- A flashlight

Once you've gathered the necessary supplies, look for two trees in your yard that are not too far apart from one another. Tie the end of the rope or twine to one tree about 5 to 6 feet above the ground. The two trees should be at least the width of the white sheet apart. Run the rope or twine to the other tree, and loop the rope around the tree at least once, ensuring the rope is level and tight. Then run the rope back to the original tree and tie it. When you're done, you'll have essentially created a clothesline.

Hang the white sheet from one rope so that the bottom of the sheet is lying on the ground. Secure the top of the sheet to the rope with the binder clips or clothespins. Pull the bottom of the sheet forward a bit creating a 90-degree angle with the ground and place a rock or brick on each bottom corner. This will help keep the sheet from flapping in the wind and allow you to observe any insects that fall off the sheet or crawl onto it from the ground.

Screw the 20-watt self-ballasted fluorescent black-light bulb into the clap light fixture. Clamp the light from the other rope so that it hangs down in front of the sheet. If using an incandescent bulb, be careful as it can get very warm. Ensure that the bulb does not contact the sheet. Turn the light on at sunset and wait for the insects to arrive. For best success, choose dark, cloudy nights and avoid times with a full moon, or a nearly full moon. Also, choose locations away from other competing artificial lights. Be patient, as it may take some time for insects to find the light. Check the sheet regularly and enjoy the many different insects that you attract. Use the plastic jar to temporarily capture and inspect individual critters.

This is a fun activity to do with a parent, another adult or older sibling. Be careful at night. Use the flashlight to light the way as you walk and wear insect repellent to avoid getting bitten by mosquitos. And most importantly, always let a parent or another adult know what you are doing.

Bug Observation Supply List

Here is a list of useful supplies to help explore and observe the hidden world of bugs in and around where you live.

- Large-mouth plastic jar with lid (used to temporarily capture bugs so that they can be safely and closed observed)

- Magnifying glass

- Forceps, plastic tweezers, or stamp tongs (for moving small objects or temporarily holding bugs)

- Long flat-head screwdriver (for probing logs or removing loose bark)

- An insect net (for collecting flying insects or sweeping through vegetation)

- Small aquarium net (for collecting insects in water)

- Small digital camera or smartphone (for taking pictures and documenting what you find)

- Mesh pop-up cage (for holding insects or rearing them)

- Binoculars (for observing from a distance)

- Small notebook (to record your observations)

- Additional insect field guides

Raising Caterpillars

Rearing butterfly or moth caterpillars is a fun way to learn about their biology. In the process, you can watch as they grow and transform from a worm-like caterpillar to a pupa or chrysalis before eventually emerging as a winged adult. As you explore and search for bugs, you will likely run across various caterpillars munching away on leaves or other plant parts. Most caterpillars are pretty easy to care for once located, but you'll need to be prepared. Here are a few basic things that you need, and remember to get your parents' permission before you start.

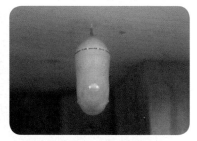

Rearing a Monarch caterpillar

WHAT YOU'LL NEED

- Garden clippers to cut plant stems or branches

- Two plastic containers with lids

- Zip-top bag with a little water in it

- Mesh pop-up cage. They are inexpensive, come in a variety of sizes and work really well.

When you find a caterpillar, note what kind of plant it was eating. This is its host plant and the food that it prefers. Most caterpillars cannot feed on just any plant. If you find a caterpillar that is not on a plant, it is probably best to just let it be.

Cut the branch, twig, or stem on which the caterpillar is feeding and place it into the plastic container. Firmly close the lid so the caterpillar cannot escape. Next, cut a few short branches, twigs or stems from the same plant. Place the vegetation in the zip-top bag making sure that the cut end goes into the water and close the bag. Make sure you remember the plant you found the caterpillar on—this will be the critical food supply for your growing caterpillar.

Take the caterpillar and the plant material home. Set up the pop-up cage. Fill a small plastic container with water and ask your parents or an adult to punch a few holes in the lid. Fill the container with water, secure the lid and place the cut end of the branches, twigs or stems through the holes into the water. For best results, ensure that the homes are just large enough to fit the stems. Place the plastic container with vegetation into the pop-up cage, gently place the caterpillar on the leaves and close the cage. Use caution. Remember that a small number of moth caterpillars have stinging or irritating hairs, so avoid handling caterpillars and instead allow them to crawl onto the fresh leaves. If you have to handle a caterpillar, its best to wear gloves. Keep the cage in an indoor location and out of direct sunlight.

Now you can watch your caterpillar eat and grow. But remember, all caterpillars are living creatures and need regular and often daily care. Just like us, they do best with clean conditions and fresh food. Plan to clean out the droppings at the bottom of the cage and add new plant material into the water each day.

Over the next several days or weeks, watch as your caterpillar eats and grows. When fully grown, they will typically stop feeding and wander to find a place to pupate or spin a cocoon. Avoid bothering the caterpillar during this time. Within a day or so, it will likely have found the perfect spot. Once the caterpillar has pupated or spun a cocoon, it may take time for an adult butterfly or moth to emerge. Keep the cage closed and check it often for an adult butterfly or moth. Once an adult has emerged, try to identify it. You may want to take a picture. After you've observed it for some time, safety let it in your yard by just opening the cage.

Moth Baiting

A moth is drawn to a baited tree.

A wide variety of moths and some other insects can be attracted to bait at night. This technique is often called sugaring or baiting and it's a great way to easily attract many cool species. There are many specific bait recipes available online, and each differs slightly in terms of ingredients. Most though include overripe fruit along with some form of sugar.

WHAT YOU'LL NEED

- A wide-mouth plastic container with lid

- Overripe fruit (you can use bananas, peaches, or apples). Since the insects are attracted by the strong smell, the more overripe or rotten the better; 1 or 2 pieces of fruit is all you'll need.

- Dark brown sugar or dark molasses (a box or small bottle)

- A wide paintbrush

- A flashlight (for spotting your finds in the dark

- A camera to get photos of the moths and other bugs you find

Put the lid on the container and place in the sun for a few hours or until the next day. Cut the fruit up into smaller chunks, and place in the plastic container. Add the dark brown sugar or molasses, and mash the ingredients together until fully mixed and the consistency of a slurry (somewhere between watery and thick).

Now find a trunk of a tree, a fence post, a boulder, a log, or a stump. Using the brush, apply the bait to the side about an hour or two before sunset. Pick a few different sites to "paint" your bait. Then check the baited area regularly through the night, and see which organisms have arrived to feed on the tasty resource.

Even a small container garden can help insects.

Planting a Pollinator Container Garden

Many insects are attracted to colorful flowers. They feed on the nectar and pollen produced or, in the case of moth and butterfly caterpillars, on the leaves or other plant parts. A container garden is a quick and relatively simply way of providing important resources for pollinators. It is also a great way of helping attract them right to your yard, deck, porch or balcony so that you can observe them more closely. While larger gardens or flowerbeds are ideal, even a container planted with flowers can attract a great variety of species.

WHAT YOU'LL NEED

- A 15- to 18-inch plastic or terracotta pot works best. Note that plastic pots are lighter and will not easily break.

- Potting soil. Any all-purpose potting mix works just fine.

- A small garden trowel. If you don't have one, a small plastic pot or container works just fine for scooping and moving soil.

- A small trellis (if including a vining plant).

- Three to five pollinator-attracting plants. Pick plants in 4-inch, 1-gallon pots. Three plants are ideal for a 15-inch pot, five for an 18-inch or larger pot. While you can pick a variety of different flowers or plants, here's a good starter list.

For nectar and pollen: Pentas (red, white, or pick colors work best), Indian Blanket, Coreopsis, Tropical Sage, Purple Trailing Lantana or other lantana, Anise Hyssop, Purple Coneflower, and Black-Eyed Susan

For caterpillars to eat: Fennel or parsley (for Black Swallowtails), Pink Swamp Milkweed or Tropical Milkweed (for Monarchs), and Corky-Stem Passionflower Vine (for Zebra Longwings and Gulf Fritillaries)

NEXT STEPS

Once you have all the materials, fill the pot about half full of potting mix. Gently remove the plants from their pots and loosen up the root system with your fingers. Place each plant in the pot. The general rule is to have the taller plants in the center or at the back. Reach the label on each plant to help figure out how tall they'll grow. For best results include one caterpillar host plant in the container. If the host plant, such as Tropical Milkweed, flowers it will attract adult pollinating insects and serve as food for hungry Monarch caterpillars.

Next, using the garden trowel or a small plastic pot, fill in around each plant's root system with soil, gently pressing it down with your hands as you go to remove any air pockets. Continue to add soil up to the top of the root mass but do not go above it. This can cause damage to the stem of the plant. Once all the soil is added, firmly tamp it down. Next, water the plants well using a garden hose or watering can. This will give them a good start. Finally, place the container in a sunny or partially sunny location. Remember to water the container regularly. Now you can enjoy for new pollinator container garden. Over the next several days and weeks, periodically watch and inspect the flowers and plants to see what insects are attracted to it.

Recommended Reading

WEBSITES

Seek by iNaturalist (www.inaturalist.org/pages/seek_app): This application uses the camera on your smartphone or tablet, along with image recognition, to help you identify insects, plants, and other organisms.

BugGuide (www.bugguide.net/node/view/15740): An online resource providing identification, images, and information on insects, spiders, and their relatives for the United States and Canada.

Butterflies and Moths of North America (www.butterfliesandmoths.org): An online resource providing information, images, and occurrence data for butterflies and moths.

FIELD GUIDES

Daniels, Jaret. *Insects & Bugs of North America: Your Way to Easily Identify Insects & Bugs* (Adventure Quick Guides). Cambridge, Minnesota: Adventure Publications, 2019.

Daniels, Jaret. *Backyard Bugs: An Identification Guide to Common Insects, Spiders, and More.* Cambridge, Minnesota: Adventure Publications, 2017.

Daniels, Jaret. *Butterflies of the Northeast: Identify Butterflies with Ease* (Adventure Quick Guides). Cambridge, Minnesota: Adventure Publications, 2019.

Daniels, Jaret. *Butterflies of the Northwest: Your Way to Easily Identify Butterflies* (Adventure Quick Guides). Cambridge, Minnesota: Adventure Publications, 2020.

Daniels, Jaret. *Butterflies of the Midwest: Identify Butterflies with Ease* (Adventure Quick Guides). Cambridge, Minnesota: Adventure Publications, 2016.

Eaton, Eric R. and Kaufman, Kenn. *Kaufman Field Guide to Insects of North America.* Boston: Houghton Mifflin Harcourt, 2007.

Evans, Arthur. *National Wildlife Federation Field Guide to Insects and Spiders & Related Species of North America.* New York: Sterling, 2007.

Evans, Arthur. *National Geographic Backyard Guide to Insects and Spiders of North America.* Washington, DC: National Geographic, 2017.

Evans, Arthur. *National Geographic Pocket Guide to Insects of North America.* Washington, DC.: National Geographic, 2016.

Phillips, David M. *Insects of North America: A Field Guide to Over 300 Insects.* New York: Falcon, 2019.

COMMUNITY SCIENCE RESOURCES

Bumblebee Watch (www.bumblebeewatch.org): A program designed to track and conserve North America's bumblebees. It relies on information collected by citizen scientists, and you can help too!

The Lost Ladybug Project (www.lostladybug.org): This program is designed to monitor ladybugs and help us better understand why some ladybug species are declining.

School of Ants (www.schoolofants.org): A program designed to study ants that live in urban areas, particularly around homes and schools.

Glossary

Abdomen The last and usually the longest or largest section of an insect's body. It contains the reproductive, digestive, and excretory systems.

Antennae Two segmented structures off the head that help with smell, taste, touch, and orientation.

Arthropods An invertebrate animal that has an external skeleton, a segmented body, and jointed appendages such as legs and antennae.

Castes Groups within a colony of social insects (such as honey bees) that look different and have different roles or functions in the colony.

Complete Metamorphosis The process by which insects that pass through four distinct stages when developing: egg, larva, pupa, and adult. (Butterflies are an example.)

Compound Eyes Large complex eyes (for vision) that are made up of hundreds of tiny individual lenses.

Desiccation To dry out due to the loss of water.

Entomology The scientific study of insects.

Exoskeleton An insect's hard (or generally hard) outer body covering, which provides protection and support.

Head The first of three main sections on an insect's body, consisting of eyes, mouthparts, and two segmented antennae.

Herbivores Organisms that feed on plants.

Incomplete Metamorphosis The process by which insects that pass through three distinct stages when developing: egg, nymph, and adult. (Grasshoppers are an example.)

Insects The largest and most diverse group of arthropods. They can be separated from other arthropods by having a three-part body consisting of a head, thorax, and abdomen.

Mouthparts Structures on the head that enable insects to feed.

Mandibles Hard, jaw-like structures of the mouth-parts that are adapted primarily for biting or chewing.

Niche The role an organism plays in the ecosystem.

Osmeterium A bad-smelling forked organ that swallowtail caterpillars can use to defend themselves.

Parasites An organism that lives on or in another organism, using it for food.

Parasitoids Organisms that live in or attach to the bodies of other organisms, primarily insects and arthropods, eventually killing them.

Predators Organisms that capture and feed on other organisms.

Proboscis The long, tongue-like mouthparts of an insect. These mouthparts are typically found in butterflies and moths and are used for sipping liquid food, such as flower nectar.

Scavengers An organism that feeds on dead organisms.

Spiracles A series of small holes along the sides of an insect's body, which it uses to breathe.

Thorax The second of three main sections of an insect's body. The thorax supports structures that enable the insect to move; these structures include three pairs of legs and one or two pairs of wings.

About the Author

Jaret C. Daniels, PhD, is a professional nature photographer, author, native plant enthusiast, and entomologist at the University of Florida, specializing in insect ecology and conservation. He has authored numerous scientific papers; popular articles; and books on gardening, wildlife conservation, and insects, including butterfly field guides for Florida, Georgia, the Carolinas, Ohio, and Michigan. His other books for Adventure Publications are *Native Plant Gardening for Birds, Bees & Butterflies: Southeast, Wildflowers of Florida Field Guide,* and *Wildflowers of the Southeast Field Guide* (the last two co-written with Stan Tekiela). Jaret lives in Gainesville, Florida, with his wife, Stephanie.